The EVERYDAY LIFE series is one of the best known and most respected of all historical works, giving detailed insight into the background life of a particular period. This edition provides an invaluable picture of prehistoric life in the Old Stone Age.

The Times Literary Supplement has commended EVERYDAY LIFE IN PREHISTORIC TIMES for its vivid narrative, admirably illustrated, and this new, revised edition is an outstanding account of how ordinary people lived before the historians left a written record of the past.

MARJORIE AND C. H. B. QUENNELL

EVERYDAY LIFE IN PREHISTORIC TIMES – THE OLD STONE AGE

Carousel Editor: Anne Wood

TRANSWORLD PUBLISHERS LTD
A National General Company

EVERYDAY LIFE IN PREHISTORIC TIMES –
THE OLD STONE AGE

A CAROUSEL BOOK 0 552 54005 6

Originally published in Great Britain
by B. T. Batsford Ltd.

PRINTING HISTORY
Batsford edition (one volume entitled *Everyday Life in
Prehistoric Times*, which forms the Carousel edition of
Everyday Life in Prehistoric Times – The Old Stone Age and
the companion Carousel volume *Everyday Life in
Prehistoric Times – The New Stone Age*) published 1959
Fifth impression 1968
Carousel edition published 1971

Revised edition © Marjorie Quennell, 1959

Carousel Books are published by Transworld
Publishers Ltd.,
Cavendish House, 57–59 Uxbridge Road,
Ealing, London, W.5

Made and printed in Great Britain by
Cox & Wyman Ltd., London, Reading and Fakenham

To
E.R.Q. and H.Q.

'The operations of the mind no doubt find their noblest expression in the language of speech, yet they are also eloquent in the achievements of the hand. The works of man's hands are his embodied thought, they endure after his bodily framework has passed into decay, and thus throw a welcome light on the earliest stages of his unwritten history.'

From *Ancient Hunters* by Prof. W. J. Sollas

PREFACE

THIS BOOK has come into being as a result of another that we wrote and illustrated. It was intended for boys and girls, and we called it a *History of Everyday Things in England*. An attempt was made to draw the eyes of our readers away from the Destruction which was to the fore in those days, and to present instead a picture of all the care and trouble which had gone to the Construction of the everyday things that were being destroyed. We gave the matter very careful consideration, and it seemed to us essential that the things illustrated should be of a type with which our readers would be familiar. Boys and girls, in their summer holidays, might have seen the Norman work at Norwich or Castle Rising, or the Renaissance work of Inigo Jones at Raynham. With some reluctance we made no mention of any earlier work. The doings of Roman, Saxon, and Dane were only hinted at, and the prehistoric period was not mentioned at all. We started with William the Conqueror, and finished at the start of the twentieth century.

Since we appear to have interested many boy and girl readers, we now want to fill in the long space before 1066. One is so apt to lump together all the earlier work, and think of it as having been done in a few centuries; the sense of perspective is lost. History is rather like travelling on the railway, the events flash past like telegraph posts, the nearer ones having their due spaces in between; but if we look back, the events, like the posts, are all bunched together and we cannot realize the spaces.

These spaces are as important as the events of History, and represent the periods when people were making up their minds; recovering perhaps from great disasters, or gathering their forces to go forward.

The races of mankind, like their works, develop by growth to flower and decay, but always there is a re-birth or renaissance. The Madeleine Art we illustrate died out in 12,000 B.C., yet still lives to inspire us; that is the boys and girls who want to do work, because if History is divided into events, and spaces, then the people are divided into those who have ideas, and want to do and make things, and the others who only deal in the ideas, and benefit by them.

Personally we hold that History is not just dates, but a long tale of man's life, labour, and achievement; and if this be so, we cannot afford to neglect the doings of prehistoric men, who with flint for their material, made all the implements and weapons they needed for their everyday life.

We call the pick-and-shovel historian an Archaeologist, from the Greek *archaios*, ancient, and *logos*, discourse. The archaeologist is helped by the astronomers and mathematicians, who are called in to decide in matters of climatic change like the Glacial Periods. A skull is found, like the one at Swanscombe in Kent, and the anatomists examine it carefully to fit it into its place as a link in the chain of man's development. The science of man and mankind is called Anthropology, from *anthropos*, a man, and *logos*, discourse. The science of life is Biology. One must also know something of geology, which is the science that deals with the structure of the earth.

Many books have been written on Prehistoric Archaeology but these are on the whole not suitable for boys and girls. We have therefore taken the ascertained and proved facts, and have plotted these out as a plan. If our readers are interested in this plan they can themselves raise a superstructure of more advanced knowledge. We do not lay claim to any great store of archaeological knowledge ourselves, and have approached our task rather as illustrators. As painter and architect, who have been making things ourselves all our lives, we may perhaps be able to treat the work of prehistoric man in a sympathetic fashion, and hope our pictures will help boys and girls to *see* these old people a little.

This brings up the question of how we are to approach prehistoric man. We must free our minds of prejudice. Some people will say that he was a loathsome creature, incredibly dirty and unpleasant. Obviously this could not have been the case with the Madeleine people, whose work we see on p. 112. There will be other people who will regard our friend as the Noble Savage, and clothe him in their minds with all the simple virtues. It will not do to jump to conclusions. Shall we judge him by his *work*? If we try to find out how he lived, the tools he used, and the things that he made with them, then in the end we shall have a picture in our own minds. This is the essential part of reading a book, that it should help us to form our own conclusions. So we do not seek to teach, nor do we wish to preach, but we do want to interest our readers, and here we give you fair warning. If we can do so; if this subtle little microbe can work its way into your system, and you want to find out how things were made and done, then you may become archaeologists yourselves.

MARJORIE AND C. H. B. QUENNELL

CONTENTS

ACKNOWLEDGEMENT

The Authors and Publishers wish to acknowledge the sources of the new line illustrations which are included in this edition:

Fig. 7 is reproduced from *Ancient Stone Implements of the British Isles* by John Evans; fig. 8 from *Man the Tool Maker* by K. P. Oakley (British Museum Natural History publication); figs. 9–12 from *The Sturge Collection* by R. A. Smith (British Museum publication); figs. 33 and 34 from *Le Préhistorique* by A. de Mortillet; figs. 35, 36 and 42–5 from *The Rock Shelter of La Colombière*, all by S. Judson and H. L. Movius; fig. 51 after E. Cartailhac; fig. 60 from *La Caverne de Niaux* by H. Breuil; fig. 61 after E. Piette; fig. 62 after E. Ray Lankester; figs. 63 and 64 from *Catalogue of Stone Age Antiquities in the British Museum*; figs. 67–9 from *Fossil Man in Spain* by H. Obermier, New Haven, 1925 (Yale University Press); fig. 70 from *Préhistoire de la Mediterranée* by M. Sauter.

LIST OF ILLUSTRATIONS

The numerals in parentheses in the text refer to the *figure numbers* of the illustrations.

List of Illustrations

BIBLIOGRAPHY

EARLY MEN

Burkitt, M. C., *The Old Stone Age* (Cambridge, 1958).

Clark, Grahame, *From Savagery to Civilization* (Cressett Press, 1947).

Coon, C. P., *Up From the Ape*.

Coon, C. P., *Why Men behave like Apes and vice-versa*.

Lamming, Annette, *Lascaux* (Penguin Books, 1959).

Leahey, L. S. B., *Adam's Ancestors* (Methuen, 1953).

Oakley, K. P., *Man the Toolmaker* (Natural History Museum, 1958).

Watson, William, *Flint Implements* (British Museum, 1959).

GENERAL PREHISTORY

Childe, V. G., *What Happened in History* (Penguin Books, 1942).

Childe, V. G., *Man Makes Himself* (Oxford, 1956).

Clark, Grahame, *Archaeology and Society* (Methuen, 1956).

Clark, Grahame, *An Outline of World Prehistory* (Cambridge, 1961).

Coon, C. P., *The Races of Europe* (Macmillan, 1939).

Davies, G. E., *The Megalith Builders of Western Europe* (Hutchinson, 1958).

LATER PREHISTORIC TIMES IN BRITAIN

Atkinson, R. J. C., *Stonehenge* (Hamilton, 1956, Penguin Books, 1960).

Bibliography

Bruce-Nutford, R., *Recent Archaeological Excavations in Britain* (Routledge, 1954).

Bulleid, A., *The Lake Villages of Somerset.*

Childe, V. G., *The Prehistory of Scotland* (Cambridge, 1935).

Clark, Grahame, *Prehistoric England* (Batsford, 1940).

Clarke, R. Rainbird, *East Anglia* (Thames & Hudson, 1959).

Fox, Sir Cyril, *The Personality of Britain* (Cardiff, National Museum of Wales, 1959).

Grimes, W. F., *The Prehistory of Wales* (Cardiff, National Museum of Wales, 1951).

Hawkes, Jacquetta, *Early Britain* (Collins, 1944).

Hawkes, Jacquetta and Christopher, *Prehistoric Britain* (Chatto, 1947, Penguin Books, 1949).

Piggott, Stuart, *Britain in Prehistory* (Oxford, 1949).

Piggott, Stuart, *Scotland Before History.*

O'Riordan, Sean, *Antiquities of the Irish Countryside* (Methuen, 1953).

Raftery, Joseph, *Prehistoric Ireland* (Batsford, 1951).

Stone, J. F. S., *Wessex Before the Celts* (Thames & Hudson, 1958).

GUIDE BOOKS

Hawkes, J. J., *A Guide to the Prehistoric and Roman Monuments in Britain and Wales* (Chatto, 1951).

Sieveking, Ann & G. de G., *A Short Guide to Caves of France and Northern Spain* (Vista Books, 1961).

Thomas, Nicholas, *A Guide to Prehistoric England* (Batsford, 1960).

HOW TO DATE BY GEOLOGY

WE SAID in our Introduction that the archaeologist is a pick-and-shovel historian. He investigates the lives of the ancient peoples by the remains which they have left behind them; he needs must dig for his information, because the very earliest times are prehistoric, and no written word remains.

When the archaeologist digs up some ancient remains, for example a single grave, or the buried foundations of a house, he may be certain that all the things in his excavation belong together. In the case of a grave they may all have belonged to a single person. This is what archaeologists call an 'association'. All the objects found in the grave are truly associated with one another in the archaeological sense. They are probably all of the same date, though some of the most beautifully made objects may be heirlooms inherited by the dead man from his father or even his grandfather. In modern times graves have gravestones with dates written upon them, and often you will see the date when a house was built carved upon it in the same manner as on a gravestone. There are all sorts of other ways in which graves or houses may be dated in historic times. They may contain coins, which can be dated accurately, or hall-marked silver, or fragments of pottery marked with the name of the maker. In the later prehistoric periods of Europe, the Neolithic, the

Bronze Age, the Iron Age, similar methods can be used, for the 'association' may contain an imported piece coming from thousands of miles away, from the ancient civilizations of the Near East and of Greece and Rome where there lived people who could read and write and calculate in terms of years. These imports – perhaps they are glass beads or wine vessels – can be dated by the archaeologist and so used to date the 'association' and perhaps a whole prehistoric people using the same sort of things as were found in the grave.

During the earliest period of Man's existence, which we call the Old Stone Age, nobody could read or write. The men of the Old Stone Age may have calculated in seasons, or even in months, from the waning of one moon to the next, but they had no means of recording their calculations.

So, when the archaeologist wishes to know how old a flint implement, or an 'association', may be he has to ask the scientist to find him a new way to calculate. Luckily for us, throughout the whole of the period of the Old Stone Age, perhaps half a million years or more, the world's climate was constantly changing from very hot to very cold, and back again. These changes are recorded in the earth's surface and geologists can date the deposits in which the changes are recorded, relative to each other, so that when we can find a stone tool in these deposits we can give it a geological date.

We must now discuss these changes in climate. They are sometimes spoken of as the Ice Age, a period when the climate of England was much colder than it is now, when the polar ice covered not only Scandinavia, but the North Sea and all of Scotland and Northern England. Actually, however, there were four Ice

Ages, all of them tens of hundreds of thousands of years long, and separated from each other by periods just as long when the climate in England was hotter than it is today and hippopotami swam in the Thames. How did this come about?

We all know that the earth revolves round the sun on a path which is called its orbit. It completes the circle in a year, and turns on its own axis in so doing once a day, or 365 times in the year. As the earth

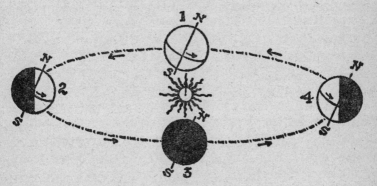

Fig. 1 Causes of the Ice Ages

turns round on its axis, the part which is towards the sun enjoys daylight, and in the part which is away it is the night.

It is quite a good plan to make a rough working model of all this on a table, as Fig. 1, and a globe will help; or let an orange take the place of the earth, and drive a knitting-needle through it for the axis. A candle in the middle of the table can be the sun. If the table is circular, the edge can be the earth's orbit; if not, a circle can be drawn in chalk. If, on this path, the knitting-needle is placed in a vertical position, so that the equator of the orange, or earth, is level with the candle, or sun, then it can be seen that the equator will derive more light from the candle than the top and bottom where the knitting-needle comes through. So we discover in the case of the earth, that the equator is hotter than the polar caps, because it gets more sunshine. If we move the orange round the orbit, turning it as we go, but keeping the knitting-needle upright, we arrive at day and night, heat and cold, but not summer and winter, or why, when we have summer, Australia has winter; but let the knitting-needle lean over, and we have an entirely different state of affairs. This is what has happened, and today the angle of inclination of the equator to the orbit of the earth is $23° 27'$. Fig. 1 shows how this affects the seasons.

The Vernal Equinox of March 21st is shown at position 1, when day and night are equal. At the Summer Solstice on June 21st, position 2, all the North Hemisphere will be turned towards the sun, and we get the longest days. At the Autumnal Equinox, September 23rd, position 3, day and night are again equal. The Winter Solstice, position 4, comes on December 21st with the shortest day, and the Northern Hemisphere leans away from the sun and warmth.

This inclination of the equator to the earth's orbit, through long ages, varies from $22° 6'$ to $24° 50'$. The former would give us less difference between winter and summer than we have now, the latter would increase the difference. The shape of the earth's orbit changes, and sometimes is roughly elliptical, with the sun much nearer to one end than the other. This would mean short summers and long cold winters.

This is what is called the Precession of the Equinoxes; the earth wobbles as it spins, and this further affects the inclination of the axis. The Gulf Stream now gives us a better climate than that to which our latitude entitles us. When we bear in mind that a very small fall in the temperature would bring back the snow and ice, then it is easy to see how a combination of the conditions we have mentioned may have caused the Ice Ages.

There is no need for alarm – thousands of years pass as the earth slowly wobbles on its journey.

The existence of these former Ice Ages was realized when geologists first began to study the places which are still in an Ice Age today, such as Switzerland. The geologists soon realized that the conditions in Switzerland had parallels in places where there is no ice today – so in order to understand the geological dating of Old Stone Age man we must go and study the glaciers in Switzerland.

A glacier is a very slowly moving river of ice. Gathering its forces from the snowfields on the summits of the mountains, it moves by gravity down the valleys, and collects tributaries as it goes along. In doing this the snow solidifies into ice, and it is quite easy to see that a tremendous pressure must be exercised on the sides of the valleys. If we go into a mountainous region, which during the Ice Age had glaciers, we shall find plenty of evidence of their existence. The sides of the valleys have been worn smooth by the slowly moving mass of ice grinding into the rocks (*roches moutonnées*); there will also be piles of splintered rocks which are called moraines. The intense cold causes the rocks above the valley to crack and splinter, and fragments fall and are left as embankments at the sides, or rolling on to the ice are carried along. These are called lateral moraines (Fig. 2(1)). Where two glaciers join, these meet, and flowing down the middle of the lower glaciers are called medial moraines (Fig. 2(2)). In this way glaciers transport materials for long distances. The débris of the lateral

Fig. 2 Glaciers and moraines

moraines falls into crevasses, or cracks in the ice, and appears lower down in the terminal moraines.

The glacier moving downhill, comes to a place where the temperature is warmer, and the ice melts. Here we find what is called a terminal moraine or moraine girdle (Fig. 2(3)). These are generally fan-shaped, and represent the heap of broken rock and stone, which has been pushed forward under the snout of the glacier, and gathered up by it in its progress from the bed and sides of the valley. The existence of old moraine girdles, which have become covered with soil and trees, and now look like hills, is a proof of ice conditions in former times. There are girdle moraines as far west as Lyons in France, which prove that the Swiss glaciers were once of enormous length. High up on the sides of valleys, the *roches moutonnées* show that the glaciers were once very much deeper. All these facts help the scientists in their conclusions as to the duration of the Ice Ages, and the temperature then general.

Behind a moraine girdle, in the bed of the old glacier, we find a sort of enormous basin, filled with hummocks of boulder clay, called drumlins, at Fig. 2(4). To make this apparent the ice of the glacier has been broken away at Fig. 2(5). This clay is the mud which was brought down by the glacier, and was formed by the churning action of its underside on the rocks over which it passed.

Below the moraine girdle, we find what the Germans call Schotter fields. It is here, where the ice melts, that the river comes into being, carrying away the smaller pieces of rock, depositing them first in the schotter, then breaking and rolling the pieces until lower down we find them in the gravel formations of the river terraces. Our readers, perhaps, will know a river whose

banks descend in terraced steps; it is a very usual
formation. This connection between the glaciers, their
girdle moraines, and river terraces is very important,
because by their aid men like Professors Geikie and
Penck have worked out the theory of the Glacial
Periods.

Professor Penck studied the River Steyr in Upper
Austria, and found that each of its terraces connected
up with the girdle moraine of an ancient glacier, and

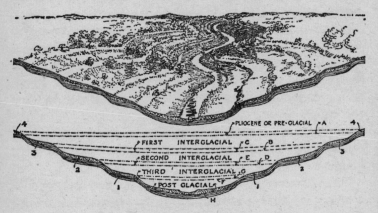

Fig. 3   The formation of river terraces

from this the following theory of the formation of
terraces themselves has been evolved. Fig. 3 has been
prepared to illustrate this.

Bed A in Fig. 3 would be pre-glacial. In the First
Glacial Period, at the end of Pliocene times, the
volume of water in the rivers would not have been
large, because so much was locked up in the ice of the
glaciers.

Then came the warmer weather of the First Interglacial Period, when vast quantities of water were
melted out of the glaciers, and hurrying down the old

river bed, or forming another, cut a new channel to B. As the water lost its power to cut channels it began to build up the bed of gravel at C.

Then came the Second Glacial Period, and the river again shrank in size. At the Second Interglacial Period the bed was cut down to D, and the bed of gravel at E built up gradually afterwards. The channel was cut down to F in Third Interglacial times, and bed G formed, and the final channel H cut in the warmer times after the Fourth Glacial Period, which we call post-glacial.

To revert to the theory of how the terraces 1, 2, and 3 were formed, we have shown the gravels of which they are composed by a dotted surface, and it will be seen that they are in reality the edges of old river-beds, which have been left behind as the water cut its way down.

Fig. 3 can be taken as showing the terraces of the Somme at St. Acheul. The Somme is celebrated, because it was here, at Abbeville, in the middle of the nineteenth century, that M. Boucher de Perthes discovered large quantities of flint implements in the gravel deposits.

At the time when this discovery was made we did not know much about the formation of river terraces, but it was realized that these flint implements must be very old indeed because they were associated in the gravels with the bones of extinct animals. As the stone tools were recognized as made by man this meant that man was himself much older than everyone thought. So that it was of great importance to date the river terraces where these stone tools had been found.

It will perhaps be as well for us now to run through the implements found in the terraces of the Somme (Fig. 3), because it will familiarize our readers with the recognized French names for the various divisions of the Old Stone Age. We have no corresponding English names, so the French ones have been very generally adopted, and these are the names of places where typical implements have been found.

No implements have been found in terraces 3 and 4, which leads us to suppose that man did not live on the banks of the Somme before the Second Interglacial Period. In the next terrace downwards, No. 2, Abbevillian implements are found. We shall explain what these are later; meanwhile, how did they get there? We have imagined a mighty river rushing down in flood at the beginning of the Second Interglacial Period, when the tremendous glaciers began to shrink and melt away, and this would be quite a different matter to the wastage only, which went on during glacial times. This flood of water is not an exaggeration. Remember that we are writing about periods which extended over, not hundreds, but thousands of years; also that we are living in an interglacial period now. In September 1920 a warm spell of a few days, accompanied by rain after a rather cold summer, caused a serious situation at Chamonix in Switzerland. The papers said a glacier had 'burst'. What really happened was that the rise in temperature caused the Mont Anvers Glacier to melt more rapidly than its accustomed rate of wastage. Masses of ice broke away, and were swept with stone and mud into the valley. Rivers rose, trees were uprooted, and houses carried away. Now think of the whole of the north of Europe under an ice-cap, and the Swiss glaciers extending as far west as Lyons in France, and the temperature gradually becoming warmer. The scientists tell us that it only wants a fall of about 5° centigrade below the mean annual temperature of Europe to have all the rigour of the glacial periods back again, or that a rise of 4° to 5° would cause all the Swiss glaciers to disappear. So that one week rather warmer than usual in the Second Interglacial Period would have wrought tremendous damage. The new river-bed would have been torn out to level B, and the first layer of gravel formed by the grinding up of the rocks and flints deposited at C. Then perhaps the winter came on or drier weather. The river shrank, and Abbeville man came down to the water's edge; he wanted to fish or drink; he may have camped there. In any case he left his tools behind and these were made of flint, and some are found today nearly as sharp and perfect as when he used them, neither rolled nor abraded. The river rose again, and bringing down more gravel covered up the tools; sometimes it carried an implement along, and bruising it very considerably in so doing deposited it lower down the river.

So man, during all the long years of the Second Interglacial Period, lived on the water's edge of the Somme, and left his tools behind him to be covered up by the gravel deposited in flood times when he had to retreat up to the higher terraces. In the gravels of this terrace are found remains of *Elephas antiquus*, a southern type of elephant which preceded the mammoth. This shows us that the climate was warm.

In the gravels of the first terrace are found later Acheulean implements, but the final gravel bed has not been explored because it is frequently submerged.

It should be noted that disturbances of the level of the earth's surface, in relation to the level of the sea, may have contributed to the formation of river terraces. For instance, well below the bed of the Thames is an old buried channel, in which the river ran when the land was higher. Any raising of the land's surface would make the river run more rapidly on its way to the sea, and so have more power to cut its way down, and form terraces, or it may have been that the Ice Age locked up tremendous quantities of water, and thus lowered the sea-level. Since Neolithic times there has been little change in the earth's surface.

Fig. 4 shows the terraces of the River Wey at Farnham, Surrey, and is included because it is nearer home than the Somme. The gravel beds are shown by solid blacks. At A no implements have been found, so this may have been the bed of an enormous river of pre-glacial times which extended as the dotted line right across the country to Hindhead. The next river

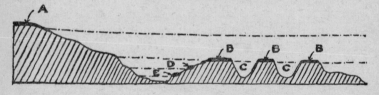

Fig. 4 The Farnham Terraces

formation was on the line B, and of this there are gravel beds remaining on three ridges, valleys between having been cut since to C. D and E show rivers which were gradually shrinking to pygmy dimensions.

It is quite easy to see that such tremendous rivers could not have existed as part of our present river system. The Thames at London meandered over 5 miles, changing course between Highbury and Clapham. Europe in Pleistocene times had a different shape, and was a bigger place than it is now, and raised higher above the sea-level. The Atlantic was perhaps 100 miles more to the west: the Mediterranean consisted of two inland seas.

The Irish Sea, English Channel, and North Sea

were wide valleys feeding noble rivers. One had for its tributaries the Thames, Rhine, and Elbe, and it discharged its waters into a northern sea just south of the Faroe Isles. Another, which we will call the River Acheulean Man, had for its tributaries the Seine, Somme, and all our southern rivers, and flowed westward to the Atlantic through the fertile *lands* of what is now the English Channel. England during some parts of the glacial periods was connected to Europe by a watershed of dry land where the Straits of Dover now are. There was an isthmus across the Mediterranean at Gibraltar, and another south of Sicily.

Before we leave the question of rivers and their terraces, we must refer back to Fig. 3. On the upper drawing of the river the gravel of the terraces, which is shown dotted, is overlain by deposits which are shown by hatched lines.

These deposits are in the nature of Loess, or loam. They are what the scientists call sub-aerial deposits, that is, deposited on the surface by the wind, as opposed to sub-aqueous, or under the action of water. The Loess, to which constant reference is made by the archaeologists, is a greyish-brown sandy and chalky loam deposited by wind in the form of dust. This was caused by the action of frost during a glacial period. As the ice retreated the earth would have been a very barren place. There is evidence that at this period there were great winds and blizzards, which swept over these deserts and blew the dust about. This frequently led to the destruction of animal life, and their bones are found now in great quantities embedded in the Loess. The position of the Loess lands is very important; beginning at the Ural Mountains they stretch across South Russia to the Carpathians and the Danube, then by way of the north-west of Austria through South Germany into the north of France. The Loess did not lend itself to the development of thick forest, so this track remained open as a route for prehistoric man from east to west. On the terrace No. 2 of the Somme at St. Acheul (Fig. 3) at its base, on the chalk, are found the gravels with the remains of *E. antiquus*, the southern elephant, and rough flint hand-axes. In the sands over the gravel are more early Abbevillian implements, and these two layers were deposited by water at the same time. Then above this start the sub-aerial deposits. First there is a white sandy loam with land shells. Above this is the older Loess in three layers, consisting of sands, and sandy loams, with gravel at base. Here are found remains of the red deer, and implements of the St. Acheul Period. Above these three layers come three others of the younger Loess, each layer divided by thin sections of gravel, in which are found Moustier implements. Above this comes brick earth, which is weathered Loess, where are found Upper Aurignac and Solutré implements, and in the soil washed down on the extreme top there are implements from the Neolithic to the Iron Age.

Think how bewildering it must have been to find all these evidences of ancient civilization in one and the same terrace, because not only were the implements found in the lowermost gravels of a later age as one went down in Fig. 3 from terrace 2 to 1, but they also were later in each terrace as one approached the surface.

Out of all these facts, the archaeologists have endeavoured to form a scale of time by which to measure the age of the peoples of the Old Stone Age and their characteristic implements. It seems a splendid picture: all these thousands of years, and man moving through them alert, resourceful, on an upward path!

2

THE EARLIEST MEN OF
THE OLD STONE AGE

WE CAN now pass to a consideration of the most interesting part of our study – prehistoric man. What did he do on the banks of the Somme, the Thames, or the Wey; how did he fend for himself, his wife, and children? Or did he first look after himself, and preach the doctrine of self-help to the family? Perhaps before we endeavour to sum up his doings, it will be well to take stock of his scanty belongings.

Having done this we shall then have to look about for a model to help us. A painter uses a dummy which he calls a lay-figure; this he dresses up and poses for the picture. In the case of prehistoric man, our model must be drawn from the savage races of modern times; and remember there are still people who use stone because they cannot work iron, but such men are few and far between now, and have lost their old self-reliance and interest by contact with civilization. Obviously we cannot draw any useful comparisons between prehistoric and civilized man; they are poles apart so far as their lives are concerned; but, if we go back a little to the earlier voyages, we can find records of people who were still living as simple and primitive a life as the prehistoric men.

The first thing to discuss, then, is the stone tools,

Fig. 5   Lower Palaeolithic man makes a flint implement

since these are nearly always the only clues we have to
the existence of the earliest men of the Stone Age.

Fig. 5 shows prehistoric man making flint implements. The ones illustrated are about $3\frac{1}{2}$ inches long.
The stone held in the right hand acted as a hammer,

and with this flakes were knocked off, and shape given to the implement. Flint flaking is an art, as can be easily tested by trying to make an implement oneself. It is a comparatively easy matter to strike off a flake, but a very difficult one to shape it. The actual idea of symmetry marks a great advance, and is the beginning of a sense of proportion; a feeling that the implement will not only cut as well as the rough flake, but that it would look better, and be more pleasant to handle, if it were shaped.

These implements would have had all kinds of uses. Flint can be made as sharp as a razor, and they served as the knives of the day, and were used to cut up a beast, scrape a bone, dig up pig-nuts, or shape a stick. Flint is extraordinarily hard – until quite recently it was used in connection with steel and tinder to produce fire. If a piece is struck against steel, minute fragments of the latter fly off, heated by the blow to such an extent that they burn in the air as sparks. Prehistoric man probably obtained his fire in this way, using, instead of steel, marcasite, an iron sulphide found in association with flint, or he may have done so by friction, rubbing one piece of wood up and down in a groove in another piece, until the dust ignited (Fig. 6).

Fig. 6   Making fire

T–B

Prehistoric man also used flints fashioned for scraping fat off the skins of the animals he killed, and the bark off all the odd pieces of wood that he must have needed. His spears would have been of wood.

Our readers will, however, agree that the early flints (Figs. 9, 10), the human origin of which is unquestioned, could not have been produced at once. Thousands of years in all probability passed before early man got into his dull head the idea of shape. At first he must have used any stick, stone, or shell that came handy. Probably happy accident came to his aid; he broke a flint and found that it had a keen cutting edge. At the identical moment that it occurred to him to turn this flint into a rough tool by trimming it into shape, he took the first step towards civilizing himself.

When man discovered the use of fire, he had an ally which not only cooked his food and warmed his body, but would at the same time have sharpened and hardened a stick of wood, so that it could be used as a spear. Put any piece of wood in a fire and char the end; when scraped it is pointed in shape.

However, there is no evidence of the use of fire before the late Acheulean, that is to say one of our latest industries in this period, so that it seems that the earliest men must have eaten their animals and vegetables uncooked and to have re-sharpened their wooden spears every time they were used.

The earliest stone tools that we really know anything about are those associated with the second terrace in the Somme Valley, described in our first chapter (Fig. 3) and with other deposits of the same age, in different parts of the world. Some of these tools are very roughly made. There are choppers made by knocking one or two flakes off a river-pebble so as to

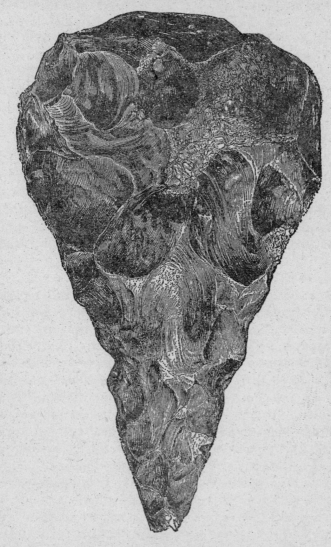

Fig. 7   Flint implement found near Gray's Inn Lane in the
seventeenth century. *After Evans*

create a sharp edge, and also tiny flakes three or four inches long. These have been found in the buried channel of the Thames in England, and also in Southern Africa. It is very difficult to believe they have been intentionally made by man, but they occur together in large numbers, in places where man had camped, and together with the more finished tools in the later deposits, so that we must accept them as the earliest tools of all.

However, we are lucky in France and England, for here, in the second terrace of the Somme, and in the Thames terrace of the same age, we have discovered the first easily recognized stone tool, which we call the hand-axe. We illustrate a number of these instruments. The first (Fig. 7) is one found in Gray's Inn Lane, London, as early as the end of the seventeenth century. It is now in the British Museum. Our beautiful engraving is from an old publication. This is quite a late (Acheulean) hand-axe. For these tools were found to be so useful that they continued to be made for more than 200,000 years, from the Second Interglacial, through the next Glacial and Interglacial Period, right up to the beginning of the last glaciation. The earliest hand-axes of the Second Interglacial Period

are known as Abbevillian hand-axes, after the site at Abbeville in the Somme Valley. Hand-axes were made by knocking flakes off a pebble or block of flint, or of some other stone if that was not available. They are usually flaked all over except at one end, where the

Fig. 8 How a flake is knocked off a flint hand-axe. *After Oakley*

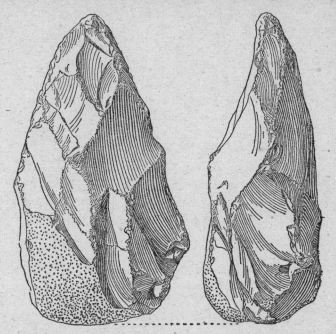

Fig. 9   Front and side view of an Abbevillian hand-axe

pebble surface is left as a hand-grip. The later, Acheulean, hand-axes, are flaked all over both sides and are much thinner and better made. Fig. 8 shows the Acheulean hand-axe and the flake which has just been knocked off. The reason why the later ones are better made is because Abbevillian man made his hand-axes by hitting them with a harder stone held in the other hand. Acheulean man discovered that if you hit the flint with a rod of wood you had more control and could make a finer flint tool. Figs. 9 and 10 show two Abbevillian hand-axes, Figs. 11 and 12 two Acheulean hand-axes. You can see that these later implements are very beautifully made. Yet experiments have shown that they can be made in a minute

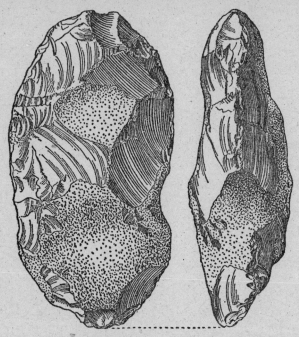

Fig. 10   Front and side view of an early
(Abbevillian) hand-axe

or two. They also get blunt very easily. At Olorgesailie, in Kenya, an Acheulean camp site has been found hidden under the sand. This is preserved so that you can go there and see the bones of the animals killed by Acheulean man still surrounded by the hand-axes he used to skin and to cut up the meat.

And if you do go there you will see that around the skeleton of one animal there may be more than twenty hand-axes and flakes. All of these have been used to skin and chop up the animal. They were thrown away when they got blunt, or when they broke in half, or just because they were too heavy to carry away. It was easier to make another hand-axe when it was required.

Many thousands of these flint implements are often found in the same gravel pit and this is thought to prove that large numbers of prehistoric people camped together. This is doubtful; food was scarce. It is, of course, always difficult to remember that an interglacial period extended over tens of thousands of years, so that if a river bank was a favourite

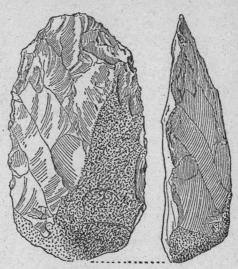

Fig. 11 Front and side view of an Acheulean hand-axe (Cleaver variety)

camping-place, the tools could have been dropped year after year, and covered up by gravel and sand in times of flood and, if these tools were so easy to make, one man in his life might have made hundreds of them. We dig these implements up today, and forget the long time which it took for the gravel to be deposited. Another point to be borne in mind is that, so far, all the remains of prehistoric man that we have noted have been found near water. The earliest men had to camp by the side of a river, or lake, because they had not any pots or pans in which to store water. Thousands of years passed before man made pottery.

We have said that the earliest hand-axes are those named after Abbeville and the later ones those named after St. Acheul, and in the last chapter we learned how these hand-axes were dated by their position in the gravels of the Somme Valley at these two small French villages. The later hand-axe people, the Acheuleans, also made another sort of tool, a heavy scraper on a large flake and in our illustration you can see a woman using one of these scrapers to cut the marrow she is eating out of a bone.

From their studies archaeologists have discovered

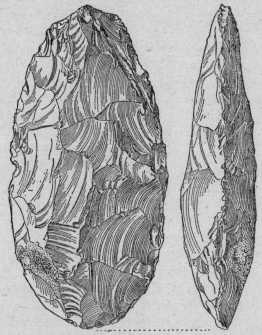

Fig. 12   Front and side view of an Acheulean hand-axe
(ovate variety)

that hand-axe man lived in many parts of the world: all over Africa and India, as well as in Western Europe, but in this book we are only going to write about them in England and France. When he lived on the banks of the Somme in France, during the Second Interglacial Period, Abbeville man had as companions

two huge eleph-
ants, *E. meridionalis*
and *E. antiquus*; the
hippopotamus,
rhinoceros, and
sabre-toothed
tiger; and a horse,
Equus stenonis. The
naturalists tell us
that the teeth of
E. antiquus were
adapted to eating
the small branches
and foliage of trees.
This gives an in-
teresting indication
of the climate. It
must have been
warm and genial
for these southern
animals to have flourished.

Fig. 13 Lower Palaeolithic scraper

How man fended for himself we cannot tell, armed
only with a hand-axe which he perhaps hafted as a
spear; he could have but little chance against an
elephant, 15 feet high to the top of the shoulder.

If looks are any criterion, the sabre-toothed tiger
Machairodus (Fig. 14) must have been an evil beast.
Machairodus was widely distributed and existed in
England with the cave men who came later on; this
we know because his teeth have been found in Kent's
Cavern, near Torquay, and Creswell Caves. Man
could only have combated such animals by craft; fire
and traps were his weapons, and one expects that he
was not too proud to eat the remains of the tiger's

feast. Fig. 15 is of a pitfall in use today by the natives of East Africa. To dig the pit would not have been beyond the wit of prehistoric man, and the stakes could have been sharpened and the points hardened by fire. Such a pit would have been a beginning of the long battle between brain and mere bulk. This would have been one way in which prehistoric man obtained the meat that he needed for his food. He was, of course, as carnivorous as his foe the tiger. He possessed neither flocks, nor herds, and did not grow any corn.

Darwin tells us that 'the Gaucho in the Pampas, for

Fig. 14 *Machairodus*, the Sabre-toothed tiger

months together, touches nothing but beef. But they eat, I observed, a very large proportion of fat.'

Again, Darwin gives us a splendid picture of how to support life, when there is not a butcher's shop just round the corner, and you have to catch your supper before you can cook it. He was in the Falkland Islands at the time. His Gaucho separated a fat cow from a herd of wild cattle, and caught it with his *lazo*. It was then hamstrung, and killed by driving a knife 'into the head of the spinal marrow'. A large circular piece of flesh was then cut out of the back, with the skin attached; this was roasted on the embers, with the hide downwards and in the form of a saucer, so that none of the gravy was lost.

Fig. 15 The pitfall

Though the weather was wet, the Gauchos managed to light their fire. First with their flint and steel they got a spark on to their piece of charred rag or tinder. Then 'they sought beneath the tufts of grass and bushes for a few dry twigs, and these they rubbed into fibres; then surrounding them with coarser twigs, something like a bird's nest, they put the rag with its spark of fire in the middle and covered it up. The nest being then held up to the wind, by degrees it smoked more and more, and at last burst out in flames.'

For fuel the Gauchos 'found what, to my surprise, made nearly as hot a fire as coals, this was the skeleton of a bullock lately killed, from which the flesh had been picked by the carrion hawks'.

The huge *Elephas antiquus* remained as a problem for the hunters to tackle. They probably employed the pitfall to trap animals – the Australians still catch emus this way – or they may have been the inventors of another device which is still employed by native races. This consists of a large and heavy piece of wood, which is suspended above a path, pointing downwards, by a grass rope. Fig. 16 shows how the animal, pushing its way along, cracks the rope, with the result that the spear falls on to the spinal column.

We may turn to Darwin to gain information as to the appearance of savage races. Writing of the Fuegians he said: 'Their only garment consists of a mantle made of guanaco skin, with the wool outside; this they wear just thrown over their shoulders.' But the skin cloak appears to have been a party frock, and not for general use. Darwin saw them in their canoes, the sleet falling and thawing on their naked bodies. He refers to the Fuegian wigwam which 'resembles, in size and dimensions, a haycock. It merely consists of a few broken branches stuck in the ground, and very imperfectly thatched on one side with a few tufts of grass and rushes. ... At Goeree Roads I saw a place where one of these naked men had slept, which absolutely offered no more cover than the form of a hare.'

Fig. 16 Falling spear

The Tasmanians

made much the same form of shelter, using bark instead of grass and rushes, and we have shown the type in Fig. 17. They also went about quite naked, using occasionally a fur cloak. Both the Fuegians and the Tasmanians liberally anointed their bodies and heads with grease mixed with the ochreous earths. In this way they gained a certain protection from the weather, and it helped to keep them clean. Earth is a fine deodorizer. There is a good tale told of a party of Tasmanians given some soup, on the top of which floated fat; this they scooped off with their hands, and put on their heads, but they did not drink the soup. Primitive man almost invariably roasts or bakes his meat.

Fig. 17   A wind-break

Later we give instances of human remains being found, buried with red ochre, for use in the spirit world. This points to the covering of grease and ochre having developed from a protection into a decoration of the body.

Darwin wrote of the Fuegians: 'The old man had a

fillet of white feathers tied round his head, which partly confined his black, coarse, and entangled hair. His face was crossed by two broad transverse bars; one painted bright red, reached from ear to ear and included the upper lip; the other, white like chalk, extended above and parallel to the first, so that even his eyelids were thus coloured.'

We have just referred to skeletons being found with colour for decorating the body, and implements for use in the spirit world, and such burials point to a belief in a future life. But we can find no traces as yet of such a belief on the part of the Abbeville man. Captain FitzRoy of the *Beagle* could never ascertain that the Fuegians had any distinct belief in a future life. When driven by extreme hunger they killed and ate the old women before their dogs, because, as they said, 'Doggies catch otters, old women no'.

We have described the sub-aerial deposits on the terraces of the Somme (p. 29). It should be noted that the earliest St. Acheul types are found in the sands and gravels at the base of the older Loess, and the later types in the upper strata. This older Loess is in three layers. It is supposed to have been deposited in glacial times; it seems as if the weather gradually became colder. This view is borne out by the remains of the animals found and in the implements. In the sand and gravel of the earlier St. Acheul times at the base of the older Loess, we have our old friend *E. antiquus* and the red deer, both southern animals; but in the older Loess itself, we meet for the first time *E. primigenius* (the mammoth), *Rhinoceros tichorhinus* (the woolly-coated one), horse, and lion. These were northern animals who came south as the weather became colder and the Fourth Glacial Period drew on.

The mammoth was not so large as *E. antiquus*, and closely resembled the existing Indian elephant, excepting only the tusks, which were very long and curved. Its teeth were more adapted for eating coarse grasses than the foliage of trees. The country was becoming barer and bleaker, and trees were scarce. Its curved tusks perhaps acted as hay-rakes, and helped to gather up food. Its warm coat and thick skin, with a layer of fat under, protected it from the cold weather. We know all about the mammoth, because whole

Fig. 18　Elephas primigenius, the mammoth

carcases have been dug up in the frozen Arctic regions, with the flesh, skin, and furry coats, protected through the ages by the ice and snow in which they were embedded. Fig. 18 gives a general idea of this animal, and Fig. 19 shows the woolly-coated rhinoceros.

It will be seen that during St. Acheul times the weather in England and France was getting colder, and as the ice-cap crept down, so these animals from the northern regions retreated before it. Man for the same reason appears to have looked about for warmer shelter than the open-air camps, and to have retreated to the caves and caverns.

Now that we have learned something about Abbeville and St. Acheul man, it would be nice to be able to say something about what he looked like. Unfortunately very few fossil human bones have been found belonging to this period. In 1891 Professor E. Dubois found the roof of a skull, two molar teeth, and a thigh-bone (femur) on the banks of the River Solo, at Trinil in Java. The position is interesting because of its relation to Australia and Tasmania. The remains were discovered in river deposit of late Pliocene, or early Pleistocene, character, and were found in conjunction with the bones of many of the lower animals of the same period; but there were no implements.

The brain-pan of Pithecanthropus exceeds that of any ape, and equals about two-thirds that of modern man. The man was long-headed or dolichocephalic. Professor G. Elliot Smith thinks that its features prove that the man belonged to the human family, and enjoyed rudimentary powers of speech. Darwin, writing of the Fuegians, said: 'The language of those people, according to our notions, scarcely deserves to be called articulate. Captain Cook has compared it to a man clearing his throat, but certainly no European ever cleared his throat with so

Fig. 19   Rhinoceros tichorhinus, the woolly-coated Rhinoceros

many hoarse, guttural, and clicking sounds.' The thighbone of Pithecanthropus shows that he walked upright, but the teeth are more simian than human. Pithecanthropus was a link between gibbon and man. He probably retreated to the trees when he was

Fig. 20 Pithecanthropus – The Java Ape-Man

alarmed, and may have contrived rough shelters or nests there, but of this, of course, we cannot be sure. The scientists went to Java because Europe was deserted by the man-like apes in early Pliocene times, when the temperature became colder. A more genial climate than ours was necessary for the development of this link which, with brain, added to bone and muscle, was to connect them with us.

It is sad that Professor Dubois could not find any tools or implements associated with Pithecanthropus.

The skull itself is what the scientists call mesaticephalic in shape, cephalic index about 78, and, as we shall be constantly meeting this and other terms used in relation to skulls, we will explain them now. The cephalic index is the ratio or percentage of the breadth of the head to the length, the latter being taken as 100.

Skulls with index of 70–75 = Dolichocephalic (long).

    ,,   ,,   ,, 75–80 = Mesaticephalic (intermediate).

Skulls with index of 80–85 = Brachycephalic (short). For example, assuming a skull has a breadth of 135 millimetres and a length of 180, we get $\dfrac{135 \times 100}{180}$ = cephalic index of 75.

A few teeth and pieces of skull-bone belonging to Pithecanthropus have also been found in China, but this man does not seem to have used hand-axes, though he belongs to the same period as these tools. The only remains of hand-axe man that we know are those found at Heidelberg in Germany and at Swanscombe in Kent.

Of the former only the jaw was found, 80 feet deep in a sand pit at Mauer, near Heidelberg. The jaw gives an impression of enormous strength, and juts out like the ram of a battleship, without any concavity to form a chin. The teeth are human, without projecting canines.

At Swanscombe in Kent gravel from an old river terrace is worked for building and other purposes. At various times implements identical with those found at St. Acheul have turned up in the Middle Gravel (layer) and it was watched with an eagle eye by an antiquary, Mr. A. T. Marston, as the workmen daily exposed more and more of that promising seam. It was not implements he hoped for, but fossil man. In June 1935 he was rewarded by a fragment of the back of a skull. If only another fragment could be found to give a missing clue! And it was, in March 1936 – part of the same skull. It can be dated with certainty to St. Acheul times and, most important, represents a type very like modern man. It is most surprising that he antedates by many thousands of years the more simian and wholly different Neanderthal man of the Mousterian period, whose acquaintance we shall make in the next chapter.

Before we pass on to the Cave-dwellers, let us sum up what we have found out about prehistoric man, and draw some comparisons. We say that he was a nomad and a hunter, but unless we are careful to think a little, the mental picture we form is of someone rather like ourselves; a little rougher perhaps, and more whiskery, but with a background of solid comfort somewhere. We shall be right in imagining the man with an active brain, but comfort as we understand it did not exist for him.

We do not realize that prehistoric man was a nomad, or wanderer, because he had to hunt for his food; that unless he hunted he starved. It is really extremely difficult to imagine a state of affairs when a man's sole possessions consisted of a flint hand-axe for a tool; a wooden spear for a weapon, and a skin for covering; when all else had to be sought; when pots and pans did not exist; when pottery and weaving had not been invented. Yet such people have existed until comparatively recent times. Tasmania was discovered in 1642, by Abel Janszoon Tasman, who named it Van Diemen's Land, after Anthony Van Diemen, the Governor of the Dutch East Indies. It has been renamed after its discoverer. After his time Tasmania was visited by other voyagers, Captain Cook being one in 1777, and they found the Tasmanians to be to all intents and purposes a palaeolithic people. It seems as if, in remote ages, when Asia, like Europe, had a different coastline, the Tasmanians had come from the mainland into Australia and, retreating again before stronger races, found their way in the end into Tasmania, before it was so much cut off as it is now. There may have been an isthmus across Bass Strait, as there was in Europe across the Straits of Dover. At some later period this disappeared, and the Tasmanians were

left free to remain the simple primitive folk they were
when first discovered.

They had not the use of iron, and their only tools
were made of flint, and very rough ones at that.
Generally the Tasmanians went about quite naked,
but on occasions wore a skin cloak. Kangaroo skins
were dressed as rugs to sit upon. Wet and cold did not
appear to harm them, and their houses (Fig. 17) were
the merest wind-breaks. When in 1831 the miserable
remainder of the natives were exiled to Flinders
Island, and lodged in huts, it was found that they
caught cold far more readily than when living in the
open. Like the Fuegians in their native state, they
greased their bodies, and anointed themselves with red
ochre; this gave a certain protection. They were also
fond of making necklaces of shells, and ornamented
their bodies by forming patterns of scars (cicatrization)
left by cuts made with a sharp flint. They were nomads
moving about the country in search of food; this
meant that in hard times the very old and infirm
people were left to die, and sometimes the babies had
to be sacrificed.

In hunting game like kangaroo they used plain
spears made of a hard wood. This is not quite the
simple thing it seems. Pithecanthropus would have
picked up any long stick to hit with, and it may have
slipped from his hand. He then discovered that unless
one end was heavier than the other, it did not follow
a very straight line of flight; it might knock down a
bird, but would not pierce with its point the skin of an
animal. So through the long ages the Tasmanian spear
developed. This was cut, trimmed, and scraped with
flint. The end was charred by fire, and so hardened,
and then pointed by scraping. The point was at the
heavy end; 20 inches from this the circumference was 3

inches, in the middle $2\frac{1}{4}$ inches, and 2 inches from the end only $\frac{1}{2}$ inch. The total length was 11 feet 11 inches. The Tasmanian could throw this and kill an animal at from 40 to 50 yards, and did not use a throwing-stick, as Fig. 26. Unlike the Australians they used neither boomerangs nor shields. Their other weapon was the waddy, or wooden club, about 2 feet 6 inches long, and they threw stones with great accuracy.

The Tasmanian wooden spear had its counterpart in England in the Old Stone Age. It is apparently the broken head, about 15 inches long, of a wooden spear, pointed at one end, and about $1\frac{1}{2}$ inches diameter at the other. It looks exactly as if the end had been broken off the Tasmanian spear and was found at Clacton in Essex, in the *E. antiquus* bed in association with an early type of flint implement. This spear-head is now exhibited in the Natural History Museum at South Kensington.

The Tasmanians were wonderful trackers, with very acute sight, hearing, and smell. They ate the animals and birds they caught. Without any preliminaries these were thrown on to a wood fire which singed the hair and feathers and half-cooked the carcase. Then the bodies were cut apart with a flint and gutted, and the cooking finished off by spitting the joints on sticks, and toasting over the fire. A little wood ash served instead of salt. The meat was always roasted, because there were not any pots to boil it in.

The Tasmanians ate shell-fish as well, and these the women caught by diving into the sea and searching the rocks under water. They did not have nets, hooks, or lines. The women were not treated very well, and had to do all the other work while the men hunted. They sat behind their lords at meals, who, reclining on one arm in Roman fashion, passed the tougher morsels to their dutiful spouses.

Fig. 21   A bark raft

The Tasmanians had one notable possession: their raft. This was not hollow like a boat, but made of cigar-shaped rolls of very light bark like cork. One large central roll had two smaller ones lashed to it with grass rope to prevent rolling (see section in Fig. 21), so that it was a raft in canoe shape. With these, or in them, they crossed from headland to headland, and the type may have been a survival of the earlier boats by which their ancestors found their way down from the mainland, and bridged the gaps between the islands, if the isthmus we referred to on p. 51 did not exist.

This raft is of great interest, because at some time or other it must have been a notable development. Pithecanthropus, if he ever went boating, did so on any floating log, and discovered to his disgust that it needed pointing, if it was to be paddled along, and also that some sort of arrangement was necessary to prevent it rolling over in the water, and giving him an involuntary bath. The beginning came in some such way. One development was the dug-out, and certain prehistoric men, with fire and flint, shaped and hollowed their log in this way.

The Tasmanian was another and very much readier method. The rafts were used for fishing, and carried three or four men comfortably; the spear, which was their only fishing implement, served as well for a pole. A clay floor was made at one end, and here a fire was lighted.

It is difficult for us to realize, with matches at hand, what a precious possession fire was to any primitive people. To obtain it they had to follow the method Darwin saw practised by the Tahitians. 'A light was procured by rubbing a blunt-pointed stick in a groove made in another, as if with the intention of deepening it, until by friction the dust became ignited' (Fig. 6). It must have been a difficult business, depending on a supply of dry moss, or fibrous bark, which could be lighted from the dust set on fire by friction. The Tasmanian then carried his fire about with him in the form of decayed touchwood, which would smoulder for hours, and could then be blown into flame.

They made grass rope and string, by twisting long wiry grass or fibrous bark (Fig. 22). This illustration is of interest, in that it leads up to the development of the spinning spindle shown in Fig. 32. Primitive man, of course, used sinews and hide thongs for ties. They also

Fig. 22 Making grass rope

made clumsy reed baskets. With a grass rope they climbed high trees. They passed the rope round themselves and the tree; cut holes in the bark for their big toes, first on one side, and then the other, and as they went up, jerked the rope and themselves up the tree together.

It is not known if they had any idea of trade or barter, but they did not grow any crops, or possess any domesticated animals.

If they ailed, an incision was made in the body, to let the pain escape. The dead were sometimes burned, and sometimes placed in hollow trees. After burning, the remains might be buried, but the skull retained and worn as a memento, or at other times this was buried separately. They believed in a life after death on a pleasant island with their ancestors.

We will finish off this account of the Tasmanians by an amusing description of one of the ways they had of settling their quarrels: 'The parties approach one another face to face, and folding their arms across their breasts, shake their heads (which occasionally come in contact) in each other's faces, uttering at the same time the most vociferous and angry expressions, until one or the other is exhausted, or his feelings of anger subside.' An extremely sensible method, and amusing for the onlookers, which is more than can be said of civilized methods of quarrelling.

It is not very creditable to the civilized white races that the Tasmanians should have been used so badly that they have now become extinct. Truganini, the last survivor, died in 1877, and, we hope, found the dream of the pleasant island and the kindly ancestors come true. A nation can die of a broken heart, even as individuals; or shall we say, they lose heart. Think of a people who have supported life with no other aid than spears, waddies, and chipped flints, then other people come in ships, with a wonderful apparatus for living, which makes the sticks and stones seem foolish and inadequate. Thus the old people lose interest, and heart, and the desire to go on living, or become hangers-on, and so come to an end.

We have written enough to prove that Abbeville and Acheul men, in their flint hand-axes, possessed tools with which they could make the spears that they needed to kill game for food; their mode of living must have been very similar to the Tasmanians. Let us now try to conjure up a picture of a tribe here in England in Abbeville and Acheul times, and find out if we can how they supported life.

The tribe was like a large family in those days. There might have been a headman, who would have been the boldest of the hunters, but little if any system of government. The women did all the work, and looked after the children, and meant more to them than the father, whose place was with the hunters. So much was this the case that the custom grew up in savage races of tracing descent on the mother's side.

The tribe would not have been particularly quarrelsome, unless their neighbours trespassed on their hunting-grounds. War is a civilized institution, based as a rule on the desire to obtain some other nation's property. Prehistoric man had little temptation in this way. Our tribe may have camped on the banks of the Wey for the summer. The river was a much bigger one than it is now, and they possibly found the fishing good. In any case they would only have had the wooden spear to lance the fish, and a flint hand-axe to cut it up afterwards. There would have been berries to eat, the roots of bracken and ferns, and nuts in the autumn, crab apples, wild cherries, and sloes. The bee had to give up his store to greedy hands that tore the comb, and crunched it up without waiting to run out the honey. There were snails and shell-fish, grubs and beetles, and luscious caterpillars.

Greatest joy of all, in the earlier age of different climatic conditions, a dead elephant, or hippo, or perhaps a rhinoceros; then would the tribe have sat down, and eaten their way through the carcase.

But rough plenty would not last; hard times and winter would come on, and the tribe range far and wide in search of food. They would grow lean-ribbed as wolves, and just as savage. They would be driven by hunger to attack living game, and in the fight some would die that the others might live. The survivors at the meal would not have presented a pleasant spectacle; they would have torn the beast to pieces, and eaten it raw.

3

THE FIRST CAVE-DWELLERS

OUR NEXT period is that of the Cave-dwellers, or Moustier men, so called after the cave of Le Moustier, in the valley of the Vézère, Dordogne. At Le Moustier the river had in course of time cut its way down through the limestone, which is left in cliff formation at the sides. In cliffs, caverns were formed by surface water finding its way down from the top through vertical joints and dissolving the rock, or by the river cutting out holes in the banks. This left the caves ready for the occupation of man, and, as the weather became colder, he looked about and found ready-made houses, a thing we should like to do today. When prehistoric man first inhabited these, they were just above the flood-level of the river; today they are often high up on the banks, because the river has continued to cut out its bed. All along the Vézère are caves, which are known all the world over by archaeologists, and later on we shall hear of La Madeleine, La Micoque, Crô-Magnon, and others.

We will start by considering Moustier man. In 1907 a skeleton was discovered in a cave on the banks of the Sourdoire, a tributary of the Dordogne, in the district of La Chapelle-aux-Saints. Let us at once point out that this is the first time we have found any evidence of people burying their dead in a place of sepulchre.

Fig. 23 Moustier cave-dwellers

The man of Java, and the man of Heidelberg, just dropped in their tracks, were brought down by the river currents, settled into the mud, and were covered up by gravel. In the case of the man of La Chapelle-aux-Saints, it is evident that he had been buried with care and perhaps love. Flint implements were laid ready to his hand for use in the hunting-grounds of the spirit world, and food for his sustenance. Think of the difference this means in the mental outlook of the relatives, and regard it as a notable step up the ladder of civilization. A similar discovery was also made at Le Moustier in 1909.

These discoveries were very important, because they enabled the archaeologists to be quite sure of their facts in respect to other skeletons which had been found. In 1856 a specimen was discovered in a limestone cave in Neanderthal, near Düsseldorf, Germany; unfortunately, the workmen who found it, not realizing its value, damaged it badly. Remember the Java man was not discovered until 1891, so the scientists were not prepared for the Neanderthaler in 1856. Some said the latter individual must have suffered from 'something on the brain', to have had such an extraordinary shape to his head, but Huxley the great Englishman and others recognized the skull as human. From time to time various other skulls were found, until that of La Chapelle-aux-Saints confirmed the opinion that all belonged to one race, which is called the Neanderthal man (*Homo Neanderthalensis*).

The most noticeable characteristic of the Moustier skull is the one very prominent ridge going right across the brows. The frontal bones are very thick, and there is not much chin to the lower jaw. The head is large in proportion to the height. The brain of the La Chapelle-aux-Saints man had a capacity of 1620 c.c.,

Fig. 24 Poise of
the Neanderthal
figure

which is about the average modern European capacity of 1550 c.c.; but in brains it is quality, not quantity, which counts. The shin and thigh bones suggest that the man stood with knees bent forward a little. The arm, again, is longer than that of modern man. It should be noticed that the head is placed on the shoulders in quite a different way from ours. If any of our readers stand with bent knees, they will find that the head and shoulders swing forward. Moustier man must have loped along, head to ground like a hunting animal, and would have found it difficult to look up.

Moustier man was widely distributed, and though he seems to have been the first to use the cave, he did not entirely desert the camping-places of his ancestors on the river banks. He is supposed to have lived at the end of the Fourth Glacial Period, so perhaps, as the weather gradually became warmer, he spent some of his summers on the Somme. Here M. Commont has identified his implements in the Ergeron, or younger Loess, which, as we have seen (p. 29), was deposited by wind on the terraces.

We had our own cave-dwellers here in England, and Kent's Cavern, one mile to the east of Torquay harbour, Devon, is well worth visiting, because it was one of their homes. Here in the water-worn passages cut out in the limestone hill, we shall find ample evidence of the occupation of man. The excavators found first a black mould deposited in historic times, then a floor of stalagmite in places 3 feet thick. Under this, reddish cave-earth, with bones of the mammoth, rhinoceros, elk, hyena, cave bear, and sabre-toothed tiger, and traces of the fires of prehistoric man.

Under the cave-earth is another floor of stalagmite, and under this again a natural concrete called breccia, in which were found the bones of the cave bear, and flint implements rougher than those discovered in the cave-earth.

The hand-axe disappeared soon after the beginning of the Moustier period; this in St. Acheul times was made by knocking flakes off a nodule of flint. The flakes were used for making small scrapers and the like. Moustier man appears to have dressed one side of his implement first on the nodule, and then to have detached it as a large flake. This, again, is an interesting fact, and shows that man was beginning to economize in the use of material. The weather, too, was becoming colder, and the hills would have been covered with snow. Flint is only found in chalk of the Cretaceous beds. In many parts of the country it has all been cut away by the action of water, and the flints taken with it to form gravel in the river terraces lower down. Flint suitable for making implements must have been valuable to prehistoric man, and a stray flint from the surface is not so good for flaking as one quarried out of chalk exposures. So for some it meant a long journey, and encounters with woolly rhinoceros *en route*, to obtain the raw material for their industry, then perhaps the bartering of skins in exchange for the flints, and a toilsome carrying home of the heavy stones. Perhaps it occurred to Moustier man that if instead of wasting a whole large flint to make one hand-axe, he used the flakes, he could make several implements out of one nodule. This is what he did, and it marks one more step up the ladder.

Levallois flakes, also used by Moustier man, are a peculiar type struck from a prepared 'tortoise' core, so that the flake has a faceted butt. Sharp-pointed flints are also found notched on one side, evidently for use as spear-heads (Fig. 25).

Spherical balls of limestone have been found, and it is thought that these may have been used as bolas. Darwin describes the bolas used by the Gauchos of Monte Video, South America. 'The bolas, or balls, are of two kinds. The simplest, which is chiefly used for catching ostriches, consists of two round stones covered with leather, and united by a thin plaited thong about 8 feet long; the

Fig. 25 Moustier spear-head

other kind differs only in having three balls united by thongs to a common centre. The Gaucho holds the smallest of the three in his hand, and whirls the other two round and round his head; then, taking aim, sends them like chain shot revolving through the air. The balls no sooner strike any object than, winding round it, they cross each other and become firmly hitched.' The Gaucho lives on horseback, but the Eskimo goes on foot, and he uses a bolas with seven or eight cords, and attached stones, and this he uses to bring down birds on the wing. The stones are formed by being knocked together till they become round.

The Reindeer and Musk Ox were new-comers from the north in Moustier times, and were hunted by prehistoric man for his food; but we do not find anything that would lead us to suppose that he had as yet domesticated animals.

There is one very black mark against the Moustier

people, and that is evidence which is supposed to point to cannibalism, contained in deposits in the Rock Shelter of Krapina, in Croatia. Here were found human bones which had been broken, as if to extract the marrow, and burnt by fire. We shall find on p. 72 that the Australian aborigines, while not being habitual cannibals, yet practised this dreadful habit, as a ceremonial way of disposing of the dead bodies of their relatives.

It will be seen from the foregoing that, though we know a little more about the Moustier men than about those of Chelles and St Acheul, it does not amount to very much. We must then search for some primitive people living under similar conditions, and at about the same stage of civilization as that of Moustier, and see if we can draw useful comparisons. The aborigines of Australia are such a people. Of them Messrs. Spencer and Gillen have written that they 'have no idea of permanent abodes, no clothing, no knowledge of any implements save those fashioned out of wood, bone, and stone, no idea whatever of the cultivation of crops, or of the laying in of a supply of food to tide over hard times, no word for any number beyond three, and no belief in anything like a supreme being'. They have not been treated quite so brutally as were the Tasmanians, and are still allowed to exist on sufferance, and end their days as a race on the unfertile lands. In the beginning, it seems as if they followed the Tasmanians into Australia from the mainland, and settled there, driving some of the latter people into Tasmania.

The Australian Aborigines' spear shows a considerable development on that of the Tasmanians, and may possibly resemble that used by the Moustier man. About 10 feet long, some have hardwood points on to which barbs were spliced. Others have a flint (Fig. 25).

Fig. 26   Australian spear-throwing

The Australians use a spear-thrower. This has many forms, but the essential feature is a stick about a yard long, with a handle at one end, and a peg at the other. Figs. 26 and 27 show the spear-thrower in use. First the end of the spear is fitted on to the peg of the thrower. This is held in the right hand well behind the body, the left hand balancing the spear. It is then thrown up and forward, the thrower imparting an additional impulse as the spear leaves the hand. Darwin when in Australia saw the natives at practice. He wrote: 'A cap being fixed at thirty yards distance, they transfixed it with a spear, delivered by the throwing-stick with the rapidity of an arrow from the bow of a practised archer.'

This short range means that the Australian must be an expert hunter and tracker, if he is to approach within striking distance of his quarry, the kangaroo. Moustier spear-throwers have not been discovered in Europe as yet, but we can safely assume that the shorter type was not arrived at without many simpler forms going before. The Australian uses a wooden shield, which is a development on the Tasmanian

equipment. Very much narrower than those of medi-
aeval times, it is a long oval in shape, varying from 2
feet to 2 feet 6 inches in length, by 6 to 12 inches in
width. Rounded on the outside, the inside of the shield
is hollowed out so as to leave a vertical handle. When
one thinks that this is all cut out of the solid with a
flint, it becomes a notable piece of work. The shield
points to quarrels and fighting, because its only purpose can be to protect the user against spear thrusts.
We do not know if the Moustier men used shields.

Our readers should pay a visit to the Ethnographical
Gallery at the British Museum, and see there a spear-
head made by an Australian in recent times, from
broken bottle-glass; it is an astonishing production, and
the man who made it a great craftsman. A visit should
also be paid to the Stone Age Room where there are
Moustier types, and so comparisons can be drawn.

The Australians make very useful knives out of long
dagger-shaped flakes of stone, and by daubing resin at
one end form rounded handles. They mount sharp

Fig. 27 Australian spear-throwing

Fig. 28 Hafting

flakes in the ends of sticks with resin, and these are used as chisels and adzes. There are stone picks inserted like the spear-heads in cleft sticks, only at right angles; these were secured with tendons and resin. Stone axes are made, and these are hafted in a withy handle, made supple by heat, and then bent around the axe, and fastened with tendons and resin.

Some of the Australian implements in the British Museum are ground and polished, and here in Europe we associate this with the next period, the Neolithic. The methods of hafting are of great interest, and pre-historic people must also have used some such way to protect their hands from the razor-like edges of the flints. Like the Tasmanians, the Australians walk abroad without any clothes, but wear skin cloaks in their huts; they stitch these together with sinew, and use bone awls and pins for piercing the skins. Necklaces and forehead bands of shells and teeth are worn, and they make themselves beautiful by pushing a short stick, called a nosepin, through the thin membrane which divides the nostrils. Their bodies are anointed with grease and red ochre. They also sacrifice joints of their little fingers, as we shall find the Aurignac men did in Europe. Their huts are very simple, and serve for the camp of a day or so, which makes a break in their wanderings. Fig. 29 shows such a type, which may have been used by Moustier man in the summer when he left his cave. It represents the next development that we should expect from the Tasmanian's wind-break (Fig. 17). It is, in fact, like two wind-breaks leaning together, and was made of any rough branches that came to hand.

The Australians have another method of lighting fires by friction: one stick is held in the hands and rotated in a hole in another, until the wood dust is ignited (Fig. 30). Darwin gives an improvement on this method: 'the Gaucho in the Pampas . . . taking a pliant stick about 18 inches long, presses one end on his breast, and the other pointed end into a hole in a piece of wood, then rapidly turns the curved part like a carpenter's centre-bit'.

Another interesting development is the bark canoe of the Australians (Fig. 31). The lines of this are much the same as that of the Tasmanians (Fig. 21), but the construction is that of a real boat, not a raft. A long strip of bark is stripped from the gum tree with a stone axe and warmed over a fire to make it supple. Curved saplings, bent as ribs, give the shape, and a stretcher goes across the tops of these, and the boat is prevented

Fig. 29 Australian hut

Fig. 30   Making fire

from spreading by grass rope ties from side to side. The prow and stern are tied up with stringy bark. A small fire is carried on a clay floor. The Australians are great fishermen, and have invented a barbed harpoon, and fish-hooks of shell and wood.

The point of the comparison is that in Europe, after Moustier times, we come across well-made harpoons, which could only have been used for fishing. These could not have developed without long experiment. Moustier man may have gone fishing with a spear without barbs, and from his poor catches may have thought out the more effective harpoon. Therefore they must have used some form of canoe, which, of course, has long since disappeared, so we turn to another primitive people for inspiration. The Australians make another form of canoe where bark is sewn on to the framework. The coracle of Wales and Ireland, the kayak and umiak of the Eskimo, were of this form, only skins were used instead of bark, and this may have been the Moustier method. We do not know that in Europe in Neolithic times the dug-out canoe was employed.

The Australians carry on trade by barter. The red ochre they need for decorating their bodies, may be exchanged for stone suitable for making implements. They have not any form of writing, but send news about by message-sticks. There is one in the British Museum from North Queensland. It resembles a short wooden lath about 3 inches long, with zigzag cuts and notches. The meaning of the message is 'that the dogs are being properly cared for, and that the writer wants clothes'. The lady would not have worn more than a skin cloak, with perhaps a hair fringe round her waist, and a necklace of shells, so that her dress allowance would not have needed to have been a very large one. The Australians are excellent hunters, as were the Tasmanians. Kangaroos are eaten, also almost all the other animals and birds, grubs and the pupæ of ants, fish and shell-fish. Their cooking is very much like that of the Tasmanians (p. 53), the animals being first gutted are cooked in a pit. All tendons are removed for use.

Another notable development is that the women collect the seeds of various grasses and plants, and grind these down between stones and winnow by pouring from one *pitchi* into another, so that the husks are blown away. They make rough cakes of the resulting flour. The *pitchi* is a shallow wooden trough used for shovel or scoop as well. The Moustier men may

Fig. 31   A bark canoe

have collected seeds in the same way, and so have started the long chain which led up to the household loaf of today. The Australian women use a yam or digging-stick, like the one illustrated (Fig. 59), but not loaded with a stone to increase weight. The yam-stick is not used to cultivate the soil, but for digging up honey ants or lizards which are eaten. Remember we have seen that Darwin found people living exclusively on meat, and that this was general before the advent of agriculture; but this collecting of seeds would naturally have suggested the idea of growing plants for food.

The Australians did not practise cannibalism, except in a ceremonial way, when, as is the case in Victoria, they regarded it as a reverent method of disposing of dead relatives.

We have seen (p. 56) that the Tasmanians made rush baskets, and grass rope for climbing trees and tying up their rafts. With the rope they would have learned the principle of twisting together short lengths of fibre, so that these made a continuous string. This is the principle of all spinning. The Arunta tribes in Central Australia can manufacture twine of fur or human hair. For this they use a spindle (Fig. 32): this is a stick about 14 inches long, which at the spinning end is pushed through holes in two thin, curved sticks, about 6 inches long, placed at right angles to one another. Some fur or hair is pulled out, and part of it twisted with the finger into a thread long enough to be tied on to the end of the spindle; this is rotated by being rubbed up or down the thigh. The remainder of the fur held in the hand is allowed to be drawn out as the spindle twists the thread; this is then wound up on to the spindle, and more of the fur paid out, and more thread twisted. This, we think, is the greatest

achievement of the Australians, and they, as we have
seen, are to all intents and purposes living in a Stone
Age. The problem is, for how long they have used the
spindle; did they bring it with them in remote ages
from the mainland; did prehistoric man, whom the
Australians so closely resemble, use a spindle? They
must have needed rope, and if they made it in this
way, then the sixteenth-century spinning-wheel, and
the eighteenth-century spinning-jenny, would have
their roots very deep in the past, because both are only
mechanically driven spindles which trace their descent
from something like Fig. 32. The Australian does not
use his twine for weaving, but contents himself with
making net bags. Fig. 22 shows a still more primitive
method of making twine out of long shreds of bark.

The Australians have a very complicated system of
relationship. A group will be divided into two classes
or phratries: one-half may be Crows, the other
Lizards. A Crow would
marry a Lizard, not
another Crow; would
be kind to all the other
Crows, and regard the
birds of that name as
feathered friends. This
was a means not only of
binding men together in
fellowship and friend-
ship, but of preserving
the decencies, and pre-
venting the marriage of
persons too closely
related for it to be
seemly. Each group had
various ceremonies,

Fig. 32   A primitive spindle

generally concerned with invoking the totem animal to promote plenty. In Aurignac times in Europe, it is suggested that the cave paintings may have had totemic significance. Totemism is very widely spread, and gives us a new respect for primitive peoples; it shows them shaping their lives to a system, and not just chattering their way along like so many monkeys.

The Australians have not any other settled form of government, but each group or tribe has a headman, who by reason of skill in hunting or special gifts takes the lead. They are not a quarrelsome people. War is a terrible luxury in which primitive man cannot afford to indulge. His quarrels are mere skirmishes as to boundaries of hunting-grounds; it never occurs to the Australian to steal his neighbour's territory. In his opinion this is inhabited by the spirits of their ancestors, and so would be a useless possession to him.

The Australians very frequently associate death not with natural causes, but with magic wrought by an enemy. This leads to trouble, because if the medicine man of the tribe names the enemy, and the enemy is a neighbour, he is tracked down and put to death. In this way the unfortunate native helps to bring about his own extinction. This fear of magic has always been strong in the minds of primitive people.

Games of all kinds are played by the children, who practise throwing spears, and also an amusing little implement called the 'weet-weet', because it has the form of a kangaroo rat. Then a day comes when the boys are grown up, and are initiated and become men. Dances are performed by the men before the novitiates to typify essential qualities. The dog and kangaroo are shown for endurance and speed. The boy has one of his front teeth knocked out to teach him to bear pain.

The bull roarer, a long flat leaf-shaped piece of wood scored across, is whirled round on a thong, and the whistling noise it makes is thought to be the voice of a god. It is the boy's introduction to the spiritual life of the tribe; to a knowledge of the Mysteries, and of the High God who lives in the Sky.

When an Australian is born it is assumed that he brings with him a *churinga*; these are long flat pieces of wood or stone with rounded ends, marked with various totem devices, and considered sacred objects. These are deposited in caves, and only brought out for ceremonies.

The Australians have various methods of disposing of their dead, but burial is the most general. With the bodies are interred weapons, food, and a drinking-cup for use in the happy hunting-grounds, so that in one more detail they resemble the Moustier man of La Chapelle-aux-Saints, with whose remains a flint hand-axe was found.

We need not continue these comparisons, but we hope that those we have given may help to build up a picture of what the surroundings of Moustier man may have been like.

At the end of the second chapter we gave a sketch of Hand-axe man, and tried to show that his most urgent need was food; that unless he hunted, he starved, and could not depend, as we do, on a shop round the corner, and the effort of other men. This was the material side of his life; but what of the spiritual? We shall be quite wrong if we think of primitive man as being only concerned with food, because man has always demanded some other interest.

We have the very early belief in a life hereafter, in the happy hunting-grounds, where conditions were kindlier, and there was more opportunity to expand. The Chapelle-aux-Saints burial, with flint implements to hand, for use in the spirit world, points to this. How did this come about? Primitive man, or woman, curled round asleep by his fire, dreamed dreams and saw visions; his spirit seemed to separate from his body, and he joined old friends who were dead, and with them followed in the chase, or did the wonderful things we all do in our dreams. When he awakened and rubbed sleepy eyes to find his own fireside, he told his friends of his adventures; that so and so was not dead but a spirit in a wonderful world. We can see the beginnings of ancestor worship. An acute fit of indigestion, coming after too much mammoth, would have provided the nightmare, and its equivalent horrors, and an underworld of bad spirits.

The man of imagination would have polished up the tale, and filled in the gaps, and gaining much renown thereby, became the medicine man or priest. He would exorcize the evil spirits, for a consideration, or bring messages from the good ones. At other times, in the excitement of hunting, the voice of the man would be echoed back from the hills, where by search he could find no other people. It was magical and mysterious, just as it was when his own face looked back at him from the pool to which he stooped to drink.

The sun, moon, and stars gave him cause for wonder, and glaciers mightier than the Baltoro seemed to him alive, as they crept to the sea. He made them gods. Perhaps on a stormy day he looked through a rift in the clouds, and saw others heaped and peaked into glittering pinnacles lighted by a sun he could not see himself, and thought of it all as the pleasant country of the land of dreams. The long nights and storms made him fearful.

4

ARTISTS OF THE OLD STONE AGE

AURIGNAC MAN

WITH MOUSTIER man the Older (Lower and Middle) Palaeolithic Period came to an end, and the next phase we shall consider will be the Upper Palaeolithic.

Two things mark the change from the earlier periods: the use of a multitude of new types of tools, all made on small blades of flint, and the arrival of Modern man (*Homo sapiens*). Blade tools are the first industrial revolution. As we have seen, some of the earliest of men's tools, the Hand-axes, were beautifully made, but you could only make one of them from a single block of flint. Mousterian tools were the same. Each time Mousterian man made a spear-head he had to knock off a large flake from a specially shaped lump of flint. If he wanted another spear-head he had to prepare another lump of flint to get the flake which he wanted. The great Upper Palaeolithic discovery was that from one block of flint you could get a great many single parallel-sided flakes. These are called blades by the archaeologist because they look like the blade of a knife. Figs. 33, 34 show the blocks of flint from which these blades were removed, called blade cores, and some blades which have been knocked off them. From each of these blades a separate flint tool could be made

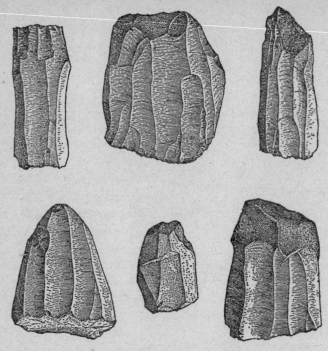

Fig. 33   Blade cores

and a great variety of these tools are found in the Upper Palaeolithic.

In fact we recognize the difference between the various people who lived in the Upper Palaeolithic by the different shapes of tool they made from these small blades. Behind the discovery of the blade tool lies another discovery. We have seen that Acheulean man found he could make thinner hand-axes by hitting a piece of flint with a wooden rod instead of battering it with another block of stone. In just the same way Upper Palaeolithic man discovered that if you took a strong pointed bone or stone rod and pressed hard enough on the flint block a narrow parallel-sided blade

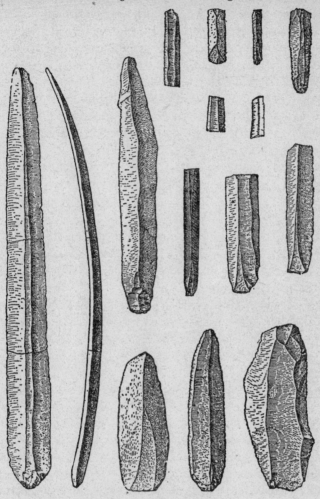

Fig. 34 Flint blades

would jump off. This is called pressure flaking. Upper
Palaeolithic man carefully shaped a block of flint to
form a cylinder or a pyramid, that is to say with one
flat end or two flat ends, as can be seen in our illustration. By pressure flaking on the very edge of the flat

end he was able to remake blades all round so that the blade core got smaller and smaller. Different sizes of blades came off the core as it got smaller, but all these could be used to make tools.

We have already said that the other important Upper Palaeolithic event was the arrival of Modern man (*Homo sapiens*). Indeed even with the first Upper Palaeolithic people known in Europe, named after Aurignac, a cave in the south of France, we already find two or three different races of prehistoric man,

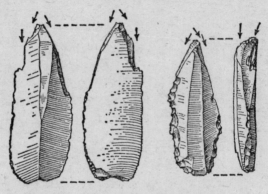

Fig. 35   Two flint burins, chisels or gravers

differing from each other as Englishman do from Frenchmen. Now, blade tools seem to have been Modern man's first discovery, and all the Upper Palaeolithic blade tools were made by Modern man. However, the earliest blade tools we know come from a cave at Mount Carmel in Palestine, where they are found mixed up with the tools of Mousterian man. In another cave at Mount Carmel, where all the tools of Mousterian man were found, the archaeologists discovered some buried human skeletons, called *Paleoanthropus Palestinus*, which seemed to belong to a mixed

race of people. In some ways they looked like Mousterian man, in some ways like *Homo sapiens*.

So that it seems that blade tools were invented in
Palestine by a special type of man who was less like
Mousterian or Neanderthal man than the sort of a man
we know today all over the world. Archaeologists are
not sure that this is quite true, but, shortly after this
important event, Modern man, carrying his blade

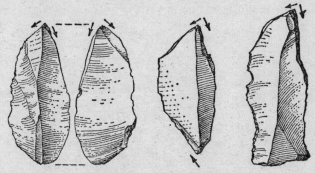

Fig. 36 Two flint burins, chisels or gravers

tools with him, spread suddenly right across Europe
and Africa and India and all the Mousterian men
disappear. So Mount Carmel provides us with an
important clue to the History of Man.

Let us now see how the earliest Modern man in
Europe lived. In France and England there are three
main peoples whom we know as Aurignac, Solutré,
and Madeleine man. They seem to have occupied the
same caves one after another so that we find their
relics in different layers in these caves, always in the
same order; the Aurignac men are always the ones in
the lowest layers and therefore the earliest occupants
of the caves.

Fig. 37 Type of huts suggested by Aurignac drawings

The Aurignac men were cave-dwellers but lived as well in the open; their camps have been found in the newer Loess (p. 30), and for this reason they have been called the Loess men. If, as has been thought, the Bushmen may be the descendants of the Aurignac men, we may perhaps assume that the Loess men had the same sort of huts. These the Bushmen constructed, much as the gipsy does today, with a framework of bent sticks covered with skins (Fig. 37). Darwin wrote of the 'toldos' of the Indians near Bahia Blanca, South America: 'These are round like ovens, and covered with hides; by the mouth of each a tapering chuzo (spear) was struck in the ground.'

The Aurignac people improved on the Moustier flint implements; we find several sorts of scrapers, knives, and gravers; the latter a tool for engraving, which must be the first tool made by man for a special purpose. These gravers or burins are very easy to recognize because of their chisel ends, shown by the arrows in our illustration. There are also scrapers, flaked ingeniously into very useful spokeshaves, and Fig. 38 shows a man shaving down the shaft for a lance. The Aurignac man, judged by the variety of tools which he possessed, must have been a clever workman making all sorts of things; remember all his woodwork has disappeared, and we only find now the imperishable flint, and some bone implements. With his burin, or graving tool, he easily cut pieces out of reindeer horns, and made arrow- and spear-heads. This use of bone marks another step forward, and from now on we shall find many examples of this new material. Bone bodkins were used to pierce skins and pass sinews through, then the bodkin had a blunt barb formed at one end to pull the thong through like a crochet-needle, and so led up to the bone needles of

Fig. 38   The spokeshave

Upper Solutré times (Fig. 47). Later on we shall find barbed harpoons. The Aurignac man used the bow and arrow – we know this because shaft-straighteners have been found, bored to take shafts of different thicknesses. These were used as shown in Fig. 39. The shaft, after having been shaved clean, would have been passed over a wood fire to make it supple, and then slipped through the hole of the shaft-straightener, which is cut obliquely. It can be seen that pressure applied on the handle would bend the shaft in any desired direction. The natives of the Punjab in India still straighten bamboos in this way, only their shaft-straightener is a substantial post set strongly in the ground. Through this there are bored holes, and the warmed bamboo is put through these, and curves removed by bending the stem in an opposite direction. The Eskimo, on the other hand, follows the Aurignac way. The early bow, like the early gun, was probably not very effective, and the spear must have remained the great weapon. Darwin, writing of the Indians from the south of Chile, said: 'The only weapon of an Indian is a very long bamboo or chuzo, ornamented with ostrich feathers, and pointed by a sharp spear-head.' The boring of holes in the shaft-straightener, and the use of the bow, suggests that the Aurignac men used the bow-drill both to bore holes and make fire, as the Eskimos do (Fig. 40).

The Aurignac men hunted for their food, as those of Le Moustier had done and people had not yet learned how to domesticate animals, or grow foodstuffs. The reindeer were very plentiful; so much is this the case that the French archaeologists talk of the Upper Palaeolithic as the Age of the Reindeer. The climate

Fig. 39 Shaft straightening

was improving, and as the Fourth Glacial Period receded, game became more plentiful. The horse was eaten in those days, and in France huge mounds of the bones have been discovered, left as the débris of many Aurignac feasts. Even as late as 1831 Darwin wrote of South American troops: 'Mare's flesh is the only food which the soldiers have when on an expedition.'

Here is an account of how the horses may have been caught, taken from Falconer's *Patagonia*: 'The Indians drive troops of wild horses into a "Corral" encompassed by high cliffs between 30 and 40 feet high, excepting at one spot where the entrance lies. This is guarded to keep them secure.'

Fig. 40   The bow-drill

At Ivinghoe Beacon there is a curious cleft in the hills, which tradition says was a wolf trap in olden days, and its form certainly lends to it the appearance of a corral.

There is another fact which goes to show that the conditions of life were becoming easier. Man and perhaps woman began to draw, and to do so extremely well. It is a most interesting fact, and one which should be noted, that the tribe was content to let these people spend their time in this way. One can imagine that the Moustier or Neanderthal man, very much occupied with the struggle for existence at the end of the Fourth Glacial Period, would have dealt sternly with the budding artist, who desired to cut his share of the 'chores', because he wanted to draw; but in Aurignac times he was allowed to do so, and drawing and sculpture extended into the Madeleine Period. These drawings and paintings are something altogether beyond the art of ordinary savage people. The Australians, for instance, decorate their wooden shields with red, white, and black, wavy lines, and lozenges, which have a pleasantly decorative effect; but of the polychrome figures which marked the culmination of Madeleine art, the Abbé Breuil has written: 'et qui place les vieux peintres des âges glyptiques bien au-dessus des animaliers de toutes les civilisations de l'orient classique et de la Grèce.' So here is another problem; it is quite certain that endless experiments must have been made before the artists could have arrived at such marvellous dexterity. How did these wonderful people jump out of the void of time? These drawings were first discovered by a Spanish nobleman, Marcellino de Santuola, who lived at Santander, Spain. He was interested in archaeology, and was digging one day in the cave of Altamira, near his home. With him was his little daughter, who, tired of watching the digging, wandered round the cave, and alarmed her father by calling out 'Toros! Toros!' Bulls in a cave would be somewhat alarming, and S. Santuola, hurrying to the rescue, found the small girl gazing at the roof of the cavern. Here he discovered drawings and paintings of bulls, bison, deer, horses, and many other animals, some life-size. The discovery threw the archaeological world into commotion – most discoveries do; people could not believe that these really wonderful drawings could have been produced at such an early stage in the world's history. Just as the Neanderthal man was not at first believed to be a man, and some early flint tools are not yet generally recognized as the work of man, so the Altamira drawings were received with scepticism. That stage has been passed through now, many books have been written, innumerable papers read before learned societies, and other drawings discovered in certain French caves, which have convinced the archaeologists that in the Altamira cave are authentic works of the earliest period of the world's art; and we owe the discovery to one small girl who called 'Toros!' in alarm to her father.

The old painters seem to have started with drawings in outline like Fig. 41, and then later in Madeleine times they passed on to solid colour, and some of these have an engraved outline. If our readers are interested

Fig. 41   Aurignac drawing

they should try to see a book by the Abbé Breuil, a distinguished Frenchman, who has made a special study of this work.

We must pass on to a consideration of what purpose the drawings served. At Altamira they are in a dark cave, which has a total length of 280 metres (a metre is about 3 feet 3⅜ inches). There is no light in the cave, and the figures occur over all the walls. They cannot be seen now without a light, and a lamp must have been used when they were painted; so we have another discovery, that man had artificial illumination in Upper Paleolithic times. A dark cave, though, does not make a good picture gallery for display, and it does not seem as if the Cave were the National Gallery of the day.

It is thought that carving in the round came first, then low relief, then outline drawing (engraving), though all these styles were no doubt contemporary for some time. Statuettes are common in Aurignac, and rare in Solutré times, and engravings reached perfection in the Madeleine period.

Many suggestions have been made as to the uses of the paintings; one is that as most of the animals drawn are those which were hunted for food, the paintings formed a magic which placed the animals under the power of the medicine man of the tribe. Many of the animals are drawn with arrows sticking in their bodies; on some the heart is shown in red. This was a practice which lingered on till recent times – to make a model of your enemy and stick it full of pins; that is, if you were a spiteful person and wished him harm.

These Aurignac drawings may therefore have been used to help the hunters. The head-man of the tribe, or perhaps the medicine man, drew an animal, and then you drew in the arrows which killed the animal. Afterwards you went out and killed a real animal brought to you by the magic of the artist. This is called Sympathetic Magic. We are also able to find the sketch-books of the artists who drew these animals on the cave walls. They are pebbles with a smooth surface where they practised their drawings. An Aurignac sketch-book only had two pages – the two sides of the pebble – so that lots of different drawings are put on top of one another on the same page. Fig. 42 shows one page of the sketch-book, with all the different drawings that have been found on it copied out separately in the

Figs. 42–45 An Aurignacian artist's sketch-book on a stone (42)

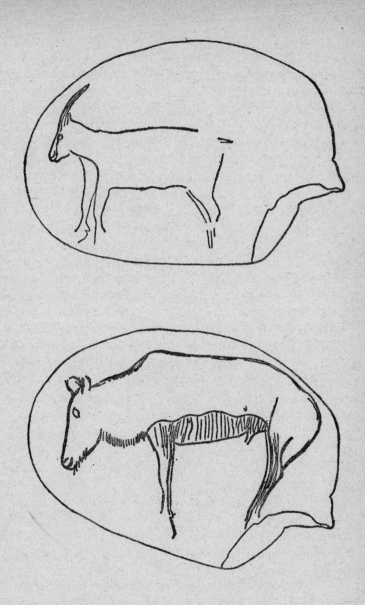

with three of the sketches drawn out separately. *After Movius*

other pictures. If you look carefully at the sketch-book you can see all these drawings.

The Aurignac men were accomplished sculptors and modelled quite good little figures in the round, about 4 to 5 inches high, and as well in low relief. A curious detail is that the faces are not rendered; in their drawings and paintings, they seldom if ever presented the human figure, except occasionally by grotesque faces. This may have arisen from the fact that primitive people think that a picture or figure of a man becomes part of his personality. If damage be done to it, then it reacts on the man, so any recognizable portrait of an individual doubles his risks. In the case of the animals drawn this was desirable to the Aurignac man.

Another suggestion is that the mammoth, the bison, or any of the animals drawn, might have been the Totem of the tribe; that they were grouped in clans, as the brothers of the bison perhaps. This, as we have seen, was a practice with the Australians, the Red Indians of America, and the boy scouts of today. The Altamira cave in this case would have been the temple in which were preserved totem symbols. One peculiarity at Altamira is that one drawing is frequently found made on the top of another. The interiors of the loftier caves must have first turned men's ideas in the direction of fine building; something which should be nobler than their little huts, and suitable for ceremonies. In the painted caves of France and Spain are found the imprints of hands. A hand has evidently been smeared with colour, and then printed on to the surface of the rock or the hand placed there first, and then colour dusted over it, leaving a white silhouette when the hand was removed. Many of the hands show traces of mutilation; that is, the end of a finger has been cut off at the joint. This dismal practice was widely spread and lasted until recent times. It was a form of sacrifice. It existed among the Australians, the Bushmen of South Africa, and some of the Red Indians, for example, and was practised for a variety of causes, generally as a sign of grief, and to implore the better favour of the gods in future. It seems reasonable, then, to suppose that the Aurignac people lost the fingers, which must have been so useful to them, in some such way.

The Aurignac women, and perhaps the men as well, appear to have been fond of trying to make themselves beautiful. Here in Great Britain, at Paviland Cave in Wales, were found perforated wolves' teeth for use as a necklace, and an ivory bracelet made by sawing rings through the hollow base of a mammoth's tusk. We can also be quite sure that so gifted a people must have experimented in the production of music. We know that they had bows and arrows. The twang of the bow led to our piano. The latter is only a harp on its side, the strings of which are struck with hammers instead of being plucked with the fingers, and the harp is the bow with many strings; the reed and pipe would lead to the horn, and the drum has always been the great instrument of the native musician. At Alpera, in Spain, are some wonderful paintings of Upper Palaeolithic date, and here are shown figures of women who seem to be dancing. Now dancing means some sort of music, and the cheerful tum-tum of a drum is almost necessary if one is to keep time. In the original Alpera drawings are figures which appear to be wearing quaint head-dresses; perhaps this was a masquerade. If all this sounds improbable, remember their wonderful drawings; to such people much is possible. Dancing has always been an accomplishment of savage people. Darwin wrote of a 'corrobery', or dancing party, of the

aborigines in Australia, held at night by the light of
fires, the women and children squatting round as
spectators. An 'Emu dance, in which each man extended his arm in a bent manner, like the neck of that
bird. In another dance, one man imitated the move-
ments of a kangaroo grazing in the woods, whilst a
second crawled up, and pretended to spear him.' In
this way they dramatized their everyday life.

SOLUTRÉ MAN

The next division of the Upper Palaeolithic is the
one which the archaeologists
have named after Solutré,
near Maçon (Saône-et-
Loire) in France. Solutré
man appears to have lived in
England, because evidences
of his industry have been
found at Paviland Cave in
South Wales, and Creswell
Crags, Derbyshire; as well
as in France, Central Europe,
and the North of Spain, but
not in Italy. The Solutré
men may have been horse
hunters who invaded Europe
along the open grasslands of
the Loess (p. 29). It has been
assumed that they were a war-
like race, because of the very
beautiful flint lance-heads
which have been found;
some of these are like an as-
segai, and would have been

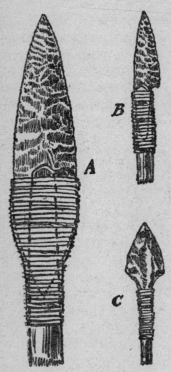

Fig. 46 Solutré flints

deadly weapons (Fig. 46). They are beautifully flaked flints, shaped like a laurel leaf, from which they get their name (*pointe en feuille de laurier*); the smaller types like a willow leaf, and so called (*pointe en feuille de saule*). B shows the highest Palaeolithic development of flint flaking, the *pointe à cran*, or shouldered point, by which a primitive barb was formed. C is an arrow-head with a flint tang which could be bound on to the shaft.

Flint flaking came to its highest point of development in the Old Stone Age in Solutré times, though it was to revive again later in the New Stone, or Neolithic Age. The Solutré people made borers, scrapers, and arrow-heads; they, in fact, carried on the Aurignac traditions; bone and ivory were used; and painting and drawing continued. Perhaps the most wonderful development of this time was the bone needle; at the beginning the sewing had been done in the same way that a shoemaker sews the sole of a shoe now, by boring a hole with a bone awl, and then passing a thread through. Of course, the Aurignac men had not any thread, but must have used fine sinews in this way. The next step was to hook the end of the awl so that the sinew could be pulled through, using the awl first to pierce the hole, and then as a crochet-needle to pull the thread through. The final step was to combine the two

Fig. 47 Making of bone needles

operations into one by the use of the needle, which pierced the hole, and carried the thread through itself (Fig. 47 (A, B, and C)). To realize the joy of a Solutré woman who first used a needle, let us imagine ourselves sewing today like a shoemaker, punching holes one at a time.

Fig. 47 shows a Solutré needlemaker at work; first she cut a splinter of bone out of reindeer horn, as at 1. This was done by cutting a groove on each side with a flint graving tool, as at 2. The splinter was then shaved down with a scraper, as 3, and polished with a piece of stone, as 4, and the eye bored with a flint borer, as 5. You can see, at the British Museum, the actual needles and the implements with which they were made. A sewing machine is a mechanically operated needle. At the British Museum you can see the start of the whole long business which led up to the sewing machine. Madeleine women later on used hollow bones as needle-cases.

Though the Fourth Glacial Period was now long past and the weather was gradually becoming more temperate, it did not improve in a regular way. The weather was colder than in Aurignac times, and the mammoth and reindeer were still found in Europe.

MADELEINE MAN

We can now pass on to the Madeleine or Magdalenian men, who succeeded those of Solutré. The typical station of the industry is on the Vézère, not far from the Castle of La Madeleine, hence the name. The Solutré man excelled in flint flaking, and the majority of the implements he made were in this material. The Madeleine man used flint for his scrapers, borers, and gravers, and finished them roughly. For other implements he made, he preferred bone and ivory. This detail at first may not seem of much importance, in reality it is as vital as if today we gave up steel and concrete and started using some new material. Flint was to have a wonderful renaissance later on in Neolithic times before it slowly gave way to bronze. In many ways the Madeleine men appear to have been the descendants of those of Aurignac.

We have said that all the Upper Palaeolithic Peoples belong to what we call Modern man. With the Early Aurignac and Solutré men it is difficult to get any idea what they looked like. The Madeleine man does occasionally draw pictures of himself, and we show one drawing that a man did of his wife all those

Fig. 48 Magdalenian portrait of a woman

years ago (Fig. 48). She is sitting down in the cave and she seems to be wearing a cape round her head, some sort of boots on her feet, and clothing rather like a boiler suit covering her from head to foot. Her nose is slightly turned up. This retroussé nose, as it is called, seems to have been a feature of some Madeleine men and women, for the newly discovered painting of a man at Angles-sur-l'Anglin has just the same feature.

Madeleine man appears to have been widely distributed over Europe. At Altamira, in Spain, he added the masterpieces of painting to the earlier drawings of the Aurignac men. He lived in France, Germany, and Belgium, and here in England his handiwork has been found at Kent's Cavern in Devon, and Creswell Crags in Derbyshire. We are so anchored nowadays, with our houses to live in, and farms to raise food-stuffs, that it is difficult to realize this widespread distribution of prehistoric man, but in reality he needed far larger areas of land on which to hunt and find food.

Madeleine man made his spear- and arrow-heads in ivory and reindeer horn; these were spliced on to wooden shafts and consisted of long lance-like points (Fig. 49(1)). From these developed harpoons, first with one row of barbs, and then with two, as Fig. 49 (2 and 3). This was a most useful discovery, that the barb would hold a fish after it had been speared; one can imagine the disgust of the early fisherman who lost his catch off the plain lance; his joy when he held it on the barbed harpoon. The first good fisherman's tale must have started with some such exploit. Spearing fish sounds a little unreal today, but there is an interesting account in Sir Walter Scott's *Redgauntlet*, of sport carried on in this way on horseback. 'They chased the fish at full gallop, and struck them with their barbed spears.' The scene is laid in the estuary of the Solway at

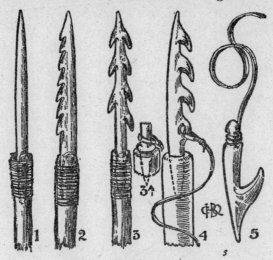

Fig. 49 Spears and harpoons

low water, when the 'waters had receded from the large and level space of sand, through which a stream, now feeble and fordable, found its way to the ocean'. Madeleine man must have had many a good day's sport like this. Out of the barb of the harpoon, the fish-hook must have developed. All this was possible in bone, though a rarity in flint. Bone lends itself to decoration, and so the Madeleine man incised simple designs on his lance-heads. Smaller bone points have been found which suggest arrow-heads, but no bows. These being wooden would have decayed. This influence of material on design is very important; it is a very false and bad art which wastes material or tortures it into a shape which is unsuitable, so these early Madeleine men were proper designers, in that they used their material in a right way. The harpoons show them to have been fishermen, and there are Madeleine drawings of seal and salmon engraved on stone and also on bone implements. We illustrate two of these drawings.

The first (Fig. 50) shows a man diving into a river, or the sea, which is full of fish. This is very poorly drawn. The second (Fig. 51) is a beautiful drawing of some seals and some snake-like fish. On the end of the two bones in this illustration you can see where the artist has drawn the harpoons with which he hopes to kill the seals. One expects that the rivers then would have been like those in Western Canada today, where the salmon come up from the sea in tremendous quantities.

Nos. 3A and 4 (Fig. 49) show another interesting development of the harpoon. Madeleine specimens have been found with a movable head, and this sug-

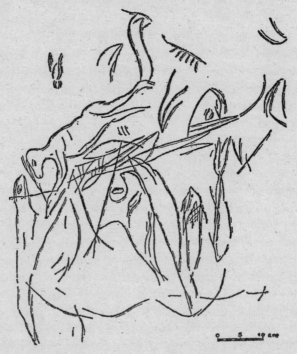

Fig. 50 A man diving into a river. Engraved on a Magdalenian bone tool

gests that they were used in the same way as the harpoons of the Eskimo. No. 5 (Fig. 49) is our suggestion of how the fish-hook developed out of the barb of the harpoon. As there are many other points of resemblance between the Eskimo and the Madeleine man, we will see if any useful comparisons can be drawn.

The Eskimos are very widely distributed, as they must be, because they live by hunting. They depend on the seal, whale, and walrus for food and clothing, and these they hunt all along the Arctic coasts from

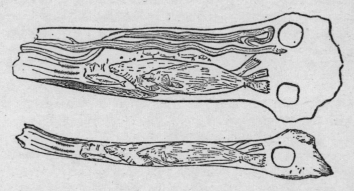

Fig. 51   Magdalenian engravings on bones of seals and fish

Greenland to Alaska. They are a very gifted, pleasant people, who have not any idea of war, because their main concern is a struggle for existence amidst ice and snow. They do not work iron, though in latter days they have made use of any pieces which they could get hold of from traders. The Eskimo works in bone and wood in a really wonderful way, as we shall see. He also appears to have inherited the skill of the Madeleine people in drawing. Dr. Nansen writes of an Eskimo from Cape York, who 'took a pencil, a thing he had never seen before, and sketched the coast-line

Fig. 52   The kayak

along Smith's Sound from his birthplace northwards
with astonishing accuracy'.

We will start with their methods of hunting. Seals
are speared at blow-holes in the ice, but far more
interesting are the methods by which they are harpooned in the open summer seas. The Eskimo uses his
kayak (Fig. 52); this is a boat which varies somewhat
in the various districts, but in all is constructed on the
same principle. On the west coast of Greenland it is
about 17 feet long, and made of driftwood on a frame
(Fig. 53), which is all bound together with thongs, and
covered with sealskin. The kayak is decked over, and
paddled with a double-bladed paddle. If we assume
that the early Madeleine men were as clever as the
Eskimos, and first made an open canoe (Fig. 31), they
would have found, as they left the rivers and ventured
to sea, that the deck was an improvement. The harpoon with movable head (Fig. 49(4)) suggests that

Fig. 53   Framework of kayak

they did go to sea, and attacked some larger quarry than the salmon. If they harpooned the seal with No. 3 (Fig. 49), the first convulsive plunge would have snapped off the head, and this was a precious possession. The head was made then to fit into a bone holder on the end of the lance, so that when the seal dived he wrenched it out of the holder only to find that it was still attached to the shaft by a leather thong. The Eskimo uses two harpoons, which are very beautiful developments of this idea.

Fig. 54(1) shows their bladder dart. The head is removable and attached by a thong to the centre of the shaft, where in addition they fix a blown-up bladder. When the seal dives he is encumbered by the shaft, which is at right angles to the thong, and the bladder, which also marks his position when he comes to the surface.

No. 2 (Fig. 54) shows the Eskimo harpoon. This had in old days an ivory head, tipped with flint, fitted on to a bone shaft. This latter is protected from snapping, by being attached to the wooden shaft with thongs in a sort of ball and socket joint. The line is attached to the ivory head, and then passes over a stud on the harpoon shaft; the loose line is carried on a holder on the kayak in front of the Eskimo, and the end is attached to a large sealskin float which rests at his back. The harpoon is propelled with

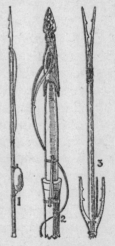

Fig. 54   Eskimo bladder dart, harpoon, and bird dart

a thrower in the same way that the Australian hurls his spears (Figs. 26, 27). The head of the harpoon buries itself in the seal, and is so attached to the line that it turns at right angles in the wound. It is at once wrenched off the bone shaft, and the position of the seal is noted by the float, which is thrown overboard. The wooden shaft floats and is picked up.

As there are many very beautiful ivory or bone har-poon-throwers of Madeleine times, it seems fair to assume that the seal was hunted then as it is by the Eskimo today.

Fig. 54(3) shows the bird dart which is used with a thrower. The forward projecting barbs kill the bird if the actual point misses. All these weapons are carried by the Eskimo on the deck of the kayak, neatly fitted under thongs and ivory studs.

The Eskimo's clothing is of sealskin, and his coat is arranged to fit closely around the circular rim of the hole in the deck in which he sits. He can be tumbled right over by a rough sea, and yet right himself with a turn of the paddle.

The Madeleine man had bone needles, and his clothing may have been like this.

At the British Museum there is a sledge made of driftwood, with bone platings on the runners, all tied up with thongs. It should be seen to realize how primi-tive man managed without nails and screws. There are also kayaks and a model of the umiak or women's boat. Fig. 55 shows an Eskimo game played rather like cup and ball. A very much simplified Polar bear is carved in ivory and pierced with many holes; the bear had to be caught through one of the holes on the end of the stick.

The boring of holes brings up the question of whether Madeleine man used the bow-drill. Small ivory rods have been found, perforated at one end, with a slit at the other shaped into a mouth. This is thought to have been the bow. The bowstring was tied through the hole at one end, given a twist round the drill, and the bow then being bent, a loop in the bow-

Fig. 55 Eskimo game

string was slipped into the notched end of the bow, and kept the latter bent. Fig. 40 shows how the drill could then be rotated. Such drills are used by the Eskimo, and many other primitive people today, both to bore holes and produce fire by friction.

Drawings have been discovered which are thought to represent tents or huts, and suggest that in Madeleine times improvements had been made on those of the Aurignac men, as shown in Fig. 37. This round beehive form, made perhaps of willow withies, would have been weak in the crown, if the tent was of any size, yet it could be constructed very simply anywhere that saplings were found. One of the Madeleine drawings suggests a type (Fig. 56). Almost all the early hut

Fig. 56   Type of huts suggested by Madeleine drawings

builders seem to have dug a hole of circular shape in the ground. The earth removed was heaped up round the outside. In the centre of the hole a roof-tree was set up, formed of the trunk of a tree, with a fork perhaps left at the top. Around this saplings were placed, their feet stuck into the surrounding mound, with the tops leaning against the roof-tree. These formed the rafters, and if in between these were interlaced smaller boughs, it is quite easy to see that the whole could be covered with skins, or rough grass thatch. Quite a comfortable little house could be made in this way, and we know that it is a type which was general in Neolithic times.

Other Madeleine drawings suggest a tepe (Fig. 75),

and this is a form of hut which is constructed by the North American Indians.

The Madeleine people had their winter quarters in caves and rock shelters, and the period is named after the rock-shelters of La Madeleine on the banks of the Vézère. Did Madeleine man, as he slowly travelled to the north, take with him a memory of the rock-shelters of France, and hand down a building tradition to the Eskimo of today? They have very interesting rock houses, and others which are constructed in a skilful way with blocks of snow. Stone lamps have been discovered, which suggest that the Madeleine man not only lighted but warmed his houses, as the Eskimo does today, by burning fat in a stone lamp with a moss wick.

Fig. 58 shows the skin tent which the Eskimo uses on his summer wanderings. The plan resembles that of the houses; there is the semicircular bed-place at A, and a central gangway at B, with cooking pots at the sides at C. The diagram shows how the tent is made with poles and covered with skins, the front portion

Fig. 57   Type of hut suggested by Madeleine drawings

being of membrane to admit light. Large stones serve to hold down the skins. We have included these drawings because we want to get as many representative types as we can of primitive dwelling-places. We shall find it useful later on.

The Madeleine man, like the Eskimo, may have used his lamp for cooking, but here is an interesting description by Darwin of some Tahitians who prepared a meal in another way: 'Having made a small

Fig. 58   Eskimo summer tent

fire of sticks, they placed a score of stones, of about the size of cricket balls, on the burning wood. In about ten minutes the sticks were consumed, and the stones hot. They had previously folded up in small parcels of leaves, pieces of beef, fish, ripe and unripe bananas, and the tops of the wild arum. These green parcels were laid in a layer between two layers of the hot stones, and the whole then covered up with earth, so that no smoke or steam could escape. In about a quarter of an hour, the whole was most deliciously cooked.' This was a method used later on in Neolithic times. The Madeleine man may have used the rein-

deer for food in the winter, by
drying the flesh over a wood fire,
and then pounding it up, and
preserving it by pouring over
hot fat, rather like the pemmican
of the Indian and Eskimo.

We cannot be sure whether
the Madeleine people had started
cultivating the soil. Perforated
stones have been found which
may have been used to load the

Fig. 59　Digging-stick

digging-stick (Fig. 59). This is the method the Bushmen adopt, and Darwin mentioned the use of the
digging-stick in Chile, to dig up roots, though this does
not mean cultivating them.

The Madeleine Period marked the highest development of the art of prehistoric man. The paintings are of
astonishing merit; without being great sticklers for
detail, these old painters caught the very spirit of the
animals they painted. The mammoth swings along
alive from the tip of his trunk to the end of his tufted
tail. The bison and boar charge; the reindeer and red
deer move in a slow, easy canter. The drawings are
proof of the immensely developed power of detailed
observation which came to the hunter as part of his
craft, and which is different from the sympathy shown
in later days, when animals were domesticated. Fig. 60
shows a bison, drawn in black and white, from a
French cave. In this drawing you can clearly see the
arrows drawn in to kill the beast.

The artists of those days used reds and browns,
blacks and yellows, and were adepts at producing high-
lights, half-tones, and shadow. They appear to have
started with a black outline, and then to have filled in

Fig. 60 A wall painting of a bison. *After Breuil*

the body of the work, adding tone, or wiping away colour to get the effect of lights. The figures are often of life size, and their vigour makes us wish that we could draw animals in such a living way.

M. Daleau has found, in France, red oxide of iron, which formed the basis of one of the colours, the pestles with which it was ground, and the shoulder-blades of animals that served as palettes. Brushes were used, and would not have been difficult to make. The paints were carried in little tubes made of reindeer horn; truly there is nothing new under the sun, and we shall find some day, perhaps, a catalogue of a Madeleine artists' colour-man. The Madeleine engravings on ivory, sometimes on the handles of their shaft-straighteners, were just as wonderful as the paintings. We have said that these artists caught the very spirit of the animals they drew, and to do this they realized that it was necessary to compose, or design, their shapes and outlines. Today we can photograph a horse while galloping, and the resulting print will not convey the sense of action that the Palaeolithic artist has obtained in Fig. 61. This is because the human eye cannot record movement with the rapidity of the lens of a camera. The artist realizes this, and presents instead a convention, or design, which we find more real than the reality of the photograph.

Remember that all the engraving and carving was done with flint implements. The engravings illustrated show deer walking across a river, and also horses' heads, drawn as if they were swimming across another river. You can see the last engraving at the British Museum, and also many others. The stone block in Fig. 64 is an artist's sketch-book with a beautifully drawn bison on it. This is also at the British Museum.

The drawings and engravings convince us that the artists knew the animals, and that their work was actual life-drawing; in this way we can find that among the Madeleine animals were mammoth, reindeer, and the great Irish deer, the bison and horse, the musk ox, glutton, and Arctic hare. These show that the

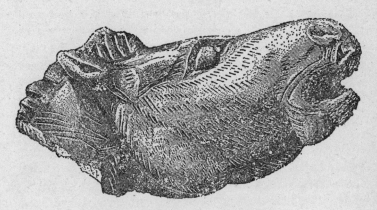

Fig. 61   The head of a galloping horse

climate was for some part of the Madeleine Period colder than in Aurignac times.

The illustrations we have given are sufficient to prove that the Madeleine people were a very highly gifted race. These people were becoming civilized, and they were artists, and so would have been pleasant and friendly. We cannot say how they said 'How do you do?' to one another; perhaps like the New Zealanders they rubbed noses. Darwin when he went there wrote: 'they then squatted themselves down and held up their faces; my companion standing over them, placed the bridge of his nose at right angles to theirs, and commenced pressing. This lasted rather longer than a cordial shake of the hand with us; and as we vary the force of the grasp of the hand in shaking, so they do in pressing. During the process they uttered comfortable little grunts.'

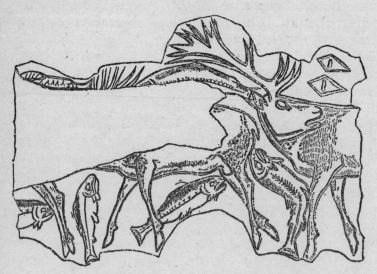

Fig. 62   Deer crossing a stream. Engraved on a round bone

Fig. 63 Three horses swimming across a stream.
Engraved on a flat rib-bone

To sum up, if it is correct that certain bone rods which have been found at Aurignac stations in France are the bows of bow-drills (Fig. 40), then this must be noted as another very considerable step forward. It is obvious that the Aurignac men must have had some ready method for drilling their shaft-straighteners (Fig. 39). The bow-drill led to the modern lathe. We shall see that in later times the people knew how to turn quite well, and it is probable that they used a type of the primitive pole lathe. In this the rotary movement was conveyed to the article to be turned by a rope which was passed around it in the same way that the bowstring was applied to the drill to turn it. The potter's wheel, which again follows later on, is descended from the bow-drill.

At the end of the third chapter we suggested that man, at first only concerned with food, had begun to realize that there was a spiritual side to his nature. In Madeleine times we find the manifestations of this in an appreciation of beauty; there were artists in those days.

Now Art is a much maligned word; it really means *doing* things, whereas science is *knowing* things. People nowadays think of an artist as a painter; we should like to define that individual as any man, or woman, who puts more into a job of work than they expect to

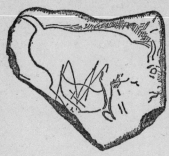

Fig. 64   A Magdalenian artist's
sketch-book

take out of it. An engineer
may be a very good artist.
A fine motor-car is a work
of Art; it has Beauty of
form, and is designed with
Truth, or it would not do
its job, so that it possesses
two of the great qualities;
there remains only Goodness.
It therefore follows that
no man can do fine work
unless he has some apprecia-
tion of the underlying principles on which humanity
has built itself up. At the very worst he can only be
one-third bad, so credit must be given to the artists of
all kinds.

We like to think that good work has been one of the
prime factors in the civilization of man, and we believe
that dull mechanical work destroys the brain.

We wonder, when our turn comes to be dug up and
have our skulls measured, say in A.D. 5000, if the
archaeologists of that far-away tomorrow will say,
Here was a people who threw away their heritage, and
arrested their development, because they lost the use
of their hands.

But so far as our friends the Madeleine men are
concerned, judged by their work they had made great
advances, and, like the Eskimo who so closely resembles them, must have been a pleasant people.

5

THE MESOLITHIC PERIOD OR
THE END OF THE OLD STONE AGE

AT THE end of the last Ice Age, when the weather
began to get warmer, the herds of horses and reindeer
followed the ice northwards towards the Polar region
and many of the Madeleine men may have followed
them. Those who remained behind in England and
France are known by other names, but are probably
the descendants of the Madeleine men and other
known tribes from nearby regions. Most of these
peoples can be recognized by their small flint arrow-
heads or microliths. These are chisel-shaped arrow-
heads used for killing small birds and animals. The
first people we know anything about in France after
the disappearance of the Madeleine men are those
named after the Cave of Mas d'Azil near Toulouse.
The Mas d'Azil men, like all these early peoples, were
widely distributed, and traces of their handiwork have
been found as far apart as the cave of Mas d'Azil,
Ariège, near Lourdes, in the south of France, and
Oban in Scotland. The Scottish discoveries of harpoons
are very interesting. They show that the ice was retreating, and man was making his way into the tracts
of the newly uncovered land.

We know what these men were like because they
had a curious habit of removing the heads from the
bodies of their dead and burying the skulls like eggs in

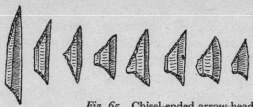

Fig. 65   Chisel-ended arrow-heads

nests. At the Ofnet Cave, near Nördlingen, Bavaria, South Germany, twenty-seven were found together buried in red ochre. This would suggest that the Mas d'Azil men used to paint their bodies in their lifetime, and so the colour was buried with them for use in the spirit world. One skull of a small child had many shells placed near it – perhaps as playthings. Round another was a chaplet of deer's teeth, and all were placed in the same way, looking westward. The actual bodies were probably consumed by fire; later cremation was a usual method, the ashes being buried in an urn.

Here is a new fact; most of the old races we have been writing about were long-headed (dolichocephalic); we now find side by side with this type, brachycephalic, or a rounder-headed people. The fact that individuals of the two races were buried in the same grave points to their having lived together happily. So that if some Madeleine people moved north after the mammoth and the reindeer, others remained behind.

We do not find any beautiful paintings in this period. Man was beginning to look on animals from a different point of view. In the old days he had the hunter's eye, quick to note beauty of body and grace of movement, which he expressed in drawings; in Mas d'Azil days he may have begun to look on himself as a herdsman, though so far only the dog was domesticated. The climate was milder, with westerly winds and warm rains; the waters were rising. Great Britain was an island, and great forests spread over the land, except where the Loess lay thick (p. 29), and by its fineness prevented the trees from taking root. Man, who had been free to roam over the tundra, was now hemmed in, so the old nomadic life passed away, and he began to have possessions.

Fig. 66   Mas d'Azil painted pebbles

These had to be useful, and we do not find any cunning work in ivory. The awl takes the place of the needle. Flint is revived for making implements, but in a rougher way than those of Solutré times. Stag horn is used for harpoons instead of reindeer horn, so the Mas d'Azil men also were fishermen.

The most interesting things which they have left behind them are the painted stones found at Mas d'Azil. These are flattish in shape, about 2 inches across, and painted with signs (Fig. 66). Some of them are surprisingly like early forms of letters – red and black were used. The use to which these stones were put is unknown, but they may have been tallies or accounts. If today you ask a labouring man to cart bricks or tiles, and keep count, he will do so in tens. These he chalks up on the barn door, and obtains his hundreds by ten tens. So these stones may have been tokens or tallies used by Mas d'Azil man in keeping

the accounts of his trade by barter. We can be quite
sure that some sort of trade had been in existence even
long before this time. In Upper Palaeolithic times
cowrie shells were found with the Crô-Magnon type of
skeleton at Laugerie-Basse. Four were near the head,
and two at each elbow, knee, and foot. They must
have been sewn on the clothing. These would have
come from the Mediterranean, and would have been
rarities in the centre of France. The chiefs would have
desired them on the principle that fine feathers, or
shells, make fine birds, or men. So, perhaps, skins or
harpoons were given in exchange. The exchange of
commodities still remains as the basis of our trade, and
we use money or bills of exchange as tallies or tokens.
Life was becoming easier, and was perhaps not so
much of a desperate struggle for survival as it had been.

The Glacial Period had receded into the past, and
the climate was temperate. Whereas in Madeleine
times the countryside had the appearance of the
Arctic tundra where the Eskimo now live, in Mas
d'Azil times it became well wooded.

Hunting tribes like the Mas d'Azil men are known
from England and Spain and also from Scandinavia
where they are the first inhabitants. During the Ice
Ages Scandinavia was, of course, entirely covered with
ice. Around the shores of the Mediterranean hunting
was still good, and paintings on rocks are known from
this period. Some of them are just as beautiful as those
painted by Madeleine man. Those we illustrate show
a deer hunt (Fig. 67), a man chasing two stags (Fig.
68), and a woman gathering honey from a bees'-nest.
The man seems to be wearing garters and feathers in
his hair, and the woman has her hair worn in a long
bob. From the south of France we also have an engraving of an ibex, but this is drawn in quite a different

style with a single line, and is not so lifelike as the older drawings.

The probable Mas d'Azil deposits at Oban were found in a cave opening on to a sea beach. On the rocky floor of the cave were successive deposits: first a pebbly gravel washed in by high tides, then a bed of

Fig. 67 A deer hunt

shells, then gravel, and on top of this another shell-bed with a final topping of black earth, formed in later ages. The level of the land has gone up, perhaps as it lost its tremendous load of ice, or that of the sea gone down, because the cave is now some 30 feet above the sea-level.

In the shell-beds are shells of oysters, limpets, whelks, the claws of lobsters, the bones of large sea fish, red deer, goat, pig, and many other animals. Ashes remain where the cooking hearths were. From

Fig. 68 A man chasing two stags

all these remains we can be quite sure that Mas d'Azil man was both fisherman and hunter, and the bones of the large sea fish mean that he took his harpoon to sea, in some form of canoe, or boat, covered with skins. Man about this time seems to have been drawn more and more to the water.

Most of the Mesolithic remains in Denmark are found in what are called Kitchen Middens. A midden is a rubbish heap, and these mounds are sometimes

100 yards long by 50 wide by 1 high, and were formed of the refuse of the meals and life of prehistoric man. They are labelled there with the splendid name of *Kjökkenmöddinger*, and are largely formed of oyster shells, with the bones of stag, roe-deer, and wild boar. The long bones have been cracked to extract the marrow. The people do not appear to have grown any crops, or domesticated any animals, except the dog, so they had not made any great advances on the civilization of the Old Stone Age. It was the pleasant loafing life of the beach-comber. The sea when it is angry casts up all kinds of edible flotsam, and in kindlier mood at low tide man could hunt over the rocks, as we do today during our summer holidays, and find lobster and crab, oyster and mussel, prawns and shrimps, and the humble winkle.

We find the remains of similar people, and their shell heaps, in different parts of the British Isles. These people possessed dug-out canoes, or skin-covered boats, with which to go fishing, and used harpoons like the Old Stone Age men. It may be that, as their flint implements were rough and not very effective, they were forced to the seaside by the encroaching forests. As the weather improved, after the Ice Ages, the trees grew, and man could not as yet make sufficient clearings in which to start agriculture.

Fig. 69 A woman gathering honey

Fig. 70   Wall painting of an ibex

The evidence that we can gain points to this dim beginning of the Mesolithic Period, some 10,000 to 12,000 years ago, as a time when the world was gathering its forces. The Old Stone Age culminated in the wonderful flint work of Solutré, and the La Madeleine paintings; after that came decline. The old hunters followed in the track of the Mammoth and the Reindeer, and reached northern latitudes, where their successors of today, the Eskimo, live. They left behind them other tribes of hunters who were able to adapt themselves to the very different condition of life along the sea-coasts and in the newly grown forests of post-ice-age Europe.

Then wise men came out of the East. There were kings in Egypt as early as 4500 B.C., and the Mediterranean, which had seen the Crô-Magnon, and Grimaldi men, in the Old Stone Age, was to see these others who, coming from the East, or South-East, in the New Stone Age, were to press along to the cry of 'Westward Ho!', and build up new civilizations.

Whether the midden people died out, or were stimulated by these new-comers we cannot be sure. They had domesticated the dog, and it may have occurred to them to do the same with other animals, and so save themselves the trouble of hunting.

In the New Stone Age man became a herdsman, and had flocks to tend. This added to his responsibilities; while as hunter, or beach-comber, his cares were few, he must have found that with possessions his troubles began. It was necessary to find pasture for the little flock, and in the winter, no matter how hard the times were, he must keep alive some few to carry on the strain; the animals needed guarding at night; better pots and pans were necessary for storing milk, and in a hundred ways he was moved to bestir and adapt himself to the new conditions which arose out of becoming a man of property.

We will now turn to the geographical conditions which confronted Neolithic man in England, and the bearing which these had on his mode of living, and the necessity that he was under of finding pasture for his flocks.

In the Old Stone Age, men walked across dry land where the Straits of Dover are now (*see* p. 29); but as the waters rose after the last Ice Age, the isthmus across got smaller and smaller, until England was completely severed. It is probable that this did not occur until some time after the beginning of the New Stone Age, and even then the Channel would not have been so wide

Fig. 71 Danish midden axe

as it is now. This was, and still is, the great Gate into England; here have passed men of the Old and New Stone Ages, Goidels, Brythons, Belgae and Romans, Saxons, Danes, and Normans. There have been, and are today, other routes, but none that can compare with the southern end of Watling Street.

We want our readers to bear in mind the physical characteristics of England; its shape; its mountains and rivers; where the watersheds and the marshy ground. Readers will remember that constant alteration has brought it to its present shape. Thanet has been an island, and the Lympne Flats under water. The Wash and Fens were unreclaimed, and the East Coast by Dunwich has been steadily eaten away; there have been alterations along the South Coast and by the Isle of Wight.

In the early Neolithic days, men could stand in Gaul and look across to Kent, and say, 'There is another land there like our own; there also can we walk dry foot on the hills, and find pasture for our beasts. The grass is growing brown here, let us go and see what the country is like.'

A drought in these early days would have led to great migrations, and the pressure from behind has forced the men on the coast to make the great adventure. The Old Testament contains the finest pictures of nomadic herdsmen. In Genesis xiii, we read how Abraham and Lot returned out of Egypt, and there was strife between their herdsmen, because the land was not able to bear them, and Abraham said to Lot, 'Is not the whole land before thee? Separate thyself, I pray thee, from me: if thou wilt take the left hand, then I will go to the right.'

INDEX

The numerals in heavy type denote the figure numbers of the illustrations